Chuck and Blanche Johnson

Savor Colorado Mountains & Western Slope Cookbook

Colorado's Finest Restaurants & Lodges Their Recipes & Their Histories

with Tracy Johnson

Wilderness Adventures Press, Inc.
Belgrade, Montana

Published by Wilderness Adventures Press, Inc.™
45 Buckskin Road
Belgrade, MT 59714
1-866-400-2012
Web site: www.wildadvpress.com
E-mail: books@wildadvpress.com
First Edition

Printed in Singapore

ISBN 1-932098-07-0
978-1-932098-07-5

Other Titles Available In This Series

Savor Denver
Savor Arizona
Savor Montana II
Savor Oregon
Savor Portland
Savor Seattle
Savor Wild Game
Savor Idaho

Table of Contents

Introduction ix
Map of Featured Restaurants xi
Colorado Facts xii

– Steamboat Springs –

L'Apogée 1
Lobster Au Gratin 3
Sizzle Salad 4
Kurobuta Pork Chops 5
Toasted Coconut Cheesecake 6
Cottonwood Grill 7
Cottonwood Shrimp and Crab Cakes 9
Sake-Lime Marinated Chilean Sea Bass 10
Hoisin Ginger Marinated Pork Tenderloin 11
Twice Roasted Chinese Five Spice Peking Duck 12

– Tabernash –

Ranch House Restaurant 15
Hot Portabella Mushroom Salad 17
Ratatouille over Polenta 18
Trout with Warm Tomato Salsa 19
Grilled Pork Chops with Berry Salsa 20
Slow Roasted Niman Ranch Tenderloin 21
Grilled Antelope with Prickly Pear Sauce 22
Swiss Tart with Colorado Peaches 23

The Wine Spectator Award 24

– Winter Park –

Gasthaus Eichler 25
Smoked Salmon Tartare 27
Spätzle 28
Veal Saltimbocca 29
Apple Strudel 30
The Shed Restaurant 31
Insalata Panzanella 33
Pan Seared Halibut 34
Tuscan Stuffed Pork Loin 35

– Keystone –

Champeaux	37
Grilled Shrimp with Marinated Tomatoes	39
Mustard-Dusted Ruby Red Trout	40
Great Northern Tavern	41
Stuffed Calamari with Chipotle Ketchup	43
Maine Lobster Meatballs	44
Mint Tea Marinated Lamb Loin	46
Dark Chocolate Pot Du Crème	47

– Breckenridge –

Briar Rose Restaurant	49
Escargot with Maitre d' Butter	51
Shrimp Calvados	52
Stuffed Colorado Striped Bass	53
Blanquette of Veal	54
Wild Mushroom Brandied Elk Tenderloins	55
Hearthstone Restaurant	57
Crab Cakes with Remoulade	59
Spice Grilled Tuna	60
Steak Au Poivre	61
Garlic Granola Crusted Elk Chop	62
Raspberry White Chocolate Bread Pudding	63
St. Bernard	65
Brie Salad	67
Seafood Cannelloni	68
Pappardelle Tartufo Bianco	69
Chicken Marsala	70

– Copper Mountain –

Alexander's on the Creek	71
Prince Edward Island Mussels	73
Pan Seared Elk Tenderloin	74
Vanilla Bean Crème Brûlée	75

– Vail –

La Tour	77
Escargot in Sauce Persillé	79
Torchon of Foie Gras	80
Dover Sole Meunière	82
Sweetbreads in Caper Brown Butter Sauce	84

Terra Bistro 87
Warm Pistachio Crusted
Haystack Mountain Goat Cheese 89
Colorado Lamb and Goat Cheese "Stroganoff" 90
Herb Marinated Bone-in Elk Loin 91

– Avon –

Beano's Cabin 93
Asparagus Soup with Truffle Oil 95
Creamy Seafood Chowder 96
Beet Marinated Salmon 96
Roast Beef Wellington 97
Mirabelle Restaurant at Beaver Creek 99
Dover Sole 101
Yellow Fin Tuna 102
Sautéed Halibut Filet 103
Sea Scallops 104
Turbotin 105
Rack of Lamb 106
Dessert Trio 107

– Carbondale –

Restaurant Six89 109
Rhubarb Martini 111
Goat Cheese Gnocchi over Field Greens 111
Grilled Pork Chops 113
Rabbit and Mushroom Ragout 114
Blueberry Corn Cakes 116
Root Beer Poached Pears 117
Maple Anglaise 118

– Aspen –

Campo de Fiori 119
Carpaccio di Bue (Beef Carpaccio) 121
Salsa alle Erbe Fini 121
Insalata Pazza 122
Farfalle al Salmone 123
Pine Creek Cookhouse 125
Seared Halibut 127
Rainbow Trout over Shiitake Salad 128
Cinnamon Dusted Elk Tenderloin 129
Jack Daniels Marinated Caribou 130

– Crested Butte –

SOUPÇON 131
Seared Hudson Valley Foie Gras 133
Pan-seared Atlantic Halibut 134
Maple Leaf Farm Duckling 134
Soupçon Crème Brûlée 136

– Montrose –

CAZWELLAS 137
Jicama Salsa 139
Grilled Pork Chop 140
Flan 141
REMINGTON'S 143
Butternut Squash Soup 145
French Bean Salad 146
Rock Shrimp and Brie Stuffed Halibut 147
Grilled Filet Mignon 149
Ginger Wild Blueberry Sorbet 151
TARRAGON AT ELK MOUNTAIN RESORT 153
Duck Cakes 155
Mushroom Onion Soup 156
Elk Mountain Mushroom Mix 157
Duck Confit 158
Pheasant Crepe 159

– Ouray –

TUNDRA RESTAURANT 161
Jumbo Lump Crab Cakes over Wilted Spinach 163
Grilled Ruby Red Trout 164
Roasted Beef Tenderloin 165

– Telluride –

9545 RESTAURANT 167
Diver Sea Scallops 169
Sake Marinated,
Apricot Kurobuta Pork Tenderloin 170
Haystack Mountain Goat
Cheese Crusted Colorado Lamb Rack 172
Croissant Bread Pudding and Apple Compote 174

– Rico –

Argentine Grille 175
Olathe Sweet Corn Bisque 177
Masa-Crusted Crisp Crab Cakes 178
Grilled "Gaucho Style" Beef Tenderloin 179

– Mancos –

Metate Room 181
Colorado Corn and Crab Cake 183
Roasted Garlic-Eggplant and Brie Soup 184
Hickory Smoked Buffalo Ribeye 185

– Durango –

East by Southwest 187
Kobe Beef-wrapped Asparagus 189
Mahi Mahi "Dorado" Ceviche 190
Chilean Sea Bass "Miso Yaki" 191
Kurobuta Pork Chop Adobo 192
Beef Teriyaki Skewers "Yakitori" 194
Berries & Choya with Ginger Ice Cream 195
The Mahogany Grille 197
Fennel and Grapefruit Salad 199
Southwestern Salmon Tamales 200
Harvest Beef Tender Stew 201
Broiled Duck Breast 202
Seasons Rotisserie & Grill 203
Butter Lettuce Salad 205
Roasted Garlic Butternut Squash Soup 206
Wild Mushroom Risotto 207
Whole Roasted Pear with Cranberry Coulis 208

About the Publishers 209
Photo Copyrights/Credits 210
Culinary Sources 211
Glossary 212
Index 214

Four women skiers at the base of the ski course in Steamboat Springs circa 1920.

Aspen between 1892 and 1897.

Introduction

One of the earliest books in our *Chuck & Blanche Johnson's Savor™ Cookbook* series is the popular *Savor Denver and Front Range Cookbook*. For those who love Colorado as much as we do, this is the companion to that book and features a prime sampling of the restaurants, their chefs and their recipes, in the rest of the state. Colorado's mountains are some of the most spectacular in the country, beckoning many to live and play in and around them. Many of the towns and villages are at challenging altitudes, making abundant fresh powder for winter recreation, as well as producing crystal clear summer days for fishing and hiking. On the western slope of the Rocky Mountains, the elevation lowers enough to produce perfect climates for agricultural pursuits; all fed by those high-mountain snow banks. For people who love to work in the restaurant trade, the mountains and western slope offer a golden opportunity to practice their vocation and live in a truly magnificent setting.

Our daughter, Tracy, has been a resident of Denver for over twelve years, and has spent much time traveling throughout Colorado. Tracy selected the restaurants in this book just as she did for the Denver book. She also provided many of the great photos you will find throughout the pages. We appreciate her help and her knowledge in producing this book as well as the help that several of her co-workers gave, especially Shelley Sale.

It is important to note that all of the featured restaurants were by invitation. None of the restaurants were charged for appearing in this book. They were selected based on the excellence and uniqueness of their food, as well as their ambience. Many have interesting histories. We also looked for places that feature comprehensive wine lists. We want to thank the owners, managers, chefs, and all the restaurant staff members who participated in getting this project to fruition.

The reader can use this book in several ways. As a travel guide, the reader can learn something about a restaurant's history, philosophy, and ambience, as well as the type of cuisine that it features. The map in the front gives the reader a perspective of the state and approximately where each restaurant is located.

Reading the recipes is a fun way to get a "taste" of each restaurant, and trying them out at home can be fun for the home chef as well as his or her guests.

Chuck and Blanche Johnson

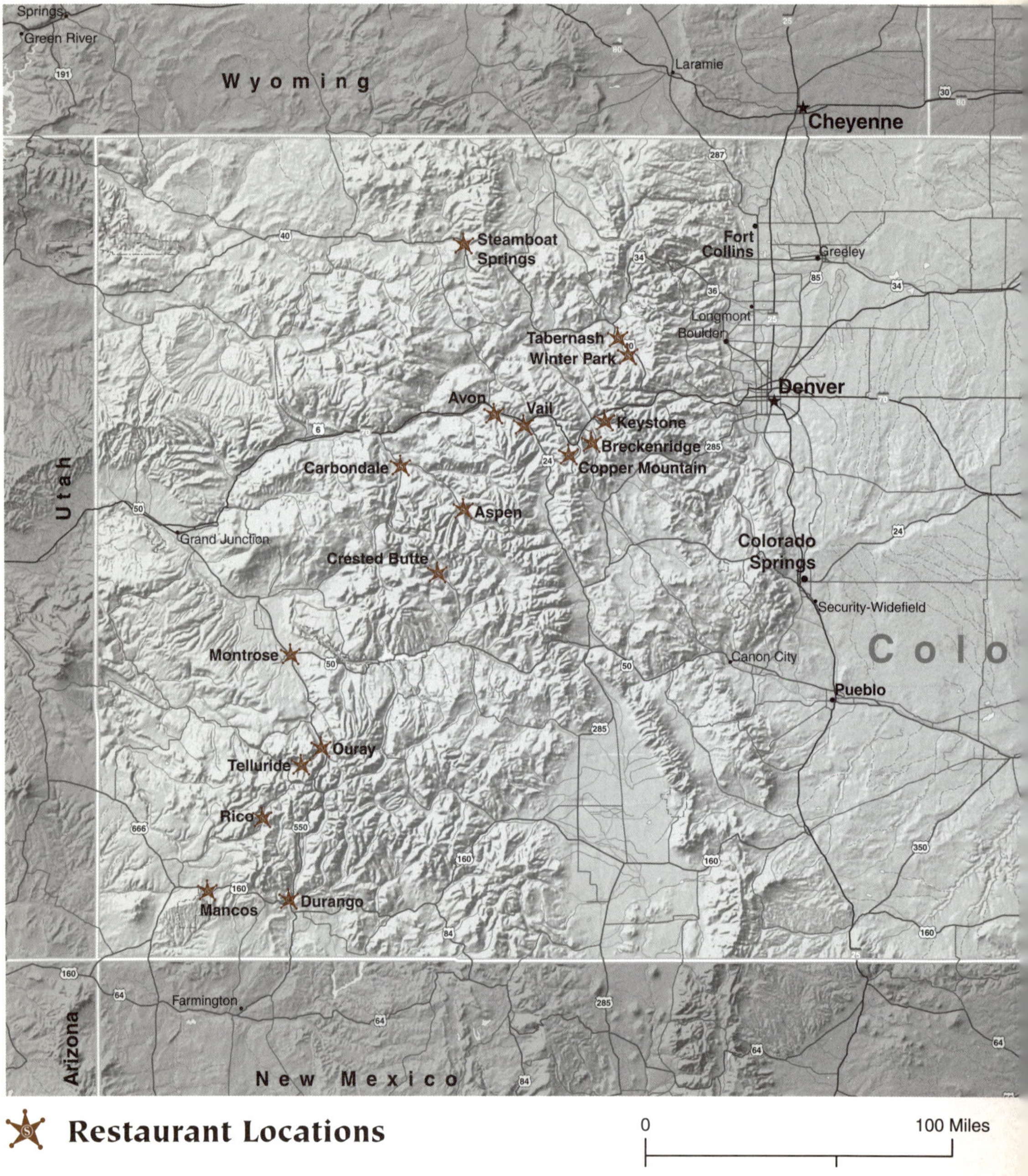
Wyoming
Utah
Arizona
New Mexico
Colo
Springs
Green River
Laramie
Cheyenne
Steamboat Springs
Fort Collins
Greeley
Longmont
Boulder
Tabernash
Winter Park
Denver
Avon
Vail
Keystone
Breckenridge
Copper Mountain
Carbondale
Aspen
Grand Junction
Colorado Springs
Crested Butte
Security-Widefield
Montrose
Canon City
Pueblo
Ouray
Telluride
Rico
Mancos
Durango
Farmington
Restaurant Locations
0
100 Miles
0
100 KM

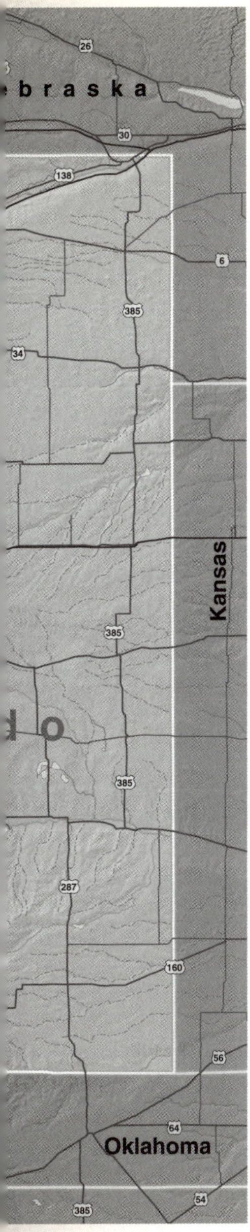

Savor Colorado Mountains & Western Slope Cookbook

Restaurants Featured

Steamboat Springs
- L'Apogée
- Cottonwood Grill
- Tabernash
- Ranch House Restaurant

Winter Park
- Gasthaus Eichler
- The Shed Restaurant

Keystone
- Champeaux
- Great Northern Tavern

Breckenridge
- Briar Rose Restaurant
- Hearthstone Restaurant
- St. Bernard

Copper Mountain
- Alexander's on the Creek

Vail
- La Tour
- Terra Bistro

Avon
- Beano's Cabin
- Mirabelle Restaurant

Carbondale
- Restaurant Six89

Aspen
- Campo de Fiori
- Pine Creek Cookhouse

Crested Butte
- Soupçon

Montrose
- Cazwellas
- Remington's
- Tarragon at Elk Mountain Resort

Ouray
- Tundra Restaurant

Telluride
- 9545 Restaurant

Rico
- Argentine Grille

Mancos
- Metate Room

Durango
- East by Southwest
- The Mahogany Grille
- Seasons Rotisserie & Grill

Colorado Facts

Admission to Statehood:
August 1, 1876
Eighth largest state in the union
104,100 square miles
380 miles east to west
280 miles north to south
Elevations - 3,315 feet to 14,433 feet
Counties - 63
Population (2000) - 4,301,261

View of a rodeo in Trinidad in 1939.

2 Indian Reservations
2 National Parks
11 National Forests
24 Wilderness Areas
11 State Parks
6 National Monuments
1 State Forest
23 State Recreation Areas
1 National Recreation Area
2 National Grasslands

Nicknames:
Centennial State
Colorful Colorado
Primary Industries:
Aerospace/Satellite
Agriculture & Food
Bioscience
Computers - Software & Storage
Capital - Denver
Bird - Lark Bunting
Animal - Bighorn sheep
Flower - Rocky Mountain Columbine
Fish - Greenback cutthroat
Tree - Blue Spruce

Hot Sulphur Springs 1899.

L'Apogée
911 Lincoln Ave.
Steamboat Springs, CO 80477
970-879-1919
www.lapogee.com
Dinner nightly: 5:00 to 11:00pm
Thai Night: Mondays –
May thru November

L'Apogée

Jamie and Sandy Jenny, Owners

Favored by locals since its opening in 1979, L'Apogée Restaurant has become a culinary icon in Steamboat Springs. The restaurant is the 2nd oldest originally owned restaurant in Steamboat. When it opened in 1979 it was located across the street from the current site. In 1985 the Jenny's purchased the building known locally as the Harwig Building. Built in 1886, the building originally housed Harwig's Saddlery and Western Wear. The restaurant is locally known as L'Apogée/Harwigs, as well as by its street number, 911. The Jenny's undertook an extensive renovation to the building, including a large wine cellar that was built underneath the restaurant to house the very extensive wine collection. In the summer, metal tables and chairs are spread out on the sidewalk in front of the building, adding a touch of Paris to the main street of Steamboat and a place for locals to socialize over a libation or to enjoy dinner al fresco.

Dinner in the main dining room of L'Apogée is an elegant affair, with candlelit tables ensconced in white linen and the soft background of live piano music. The cuisine is a combination of classic French offerings, such as French Onion Soup, Escargot, and Roast Duck, and Asian Fusion, as enjoyed in the Scallops RH, diver scallops seared in olive oil and garnished with Asian pear batons and Madras curry vinaigrette. The Asian influence has become very popular with the guests, and has resulted in a special Thai Night every Monday during the months of May through November. A separate menu is available only on these nights and features a large list of mouthwatering Asian delights.

Enophile, Jamie Jenny, has amassed an outstanding wine cellar with the customer as his primary focus. His wine philosophy is that moderate pricing is just as important to the wine experience as is the extent of the list. The emphasis is on matching the wines with the culinary offerings of the restaurant, as well as satisfying the curiosity of most wine lovers. Along with the belowground wine cellar, he also has a temperature-controlled room for the white wines on the ground floor. A special wine dispensing system allows the restaurant to serve over thirty vintage wines by the glass, including some of the finest older bottles from the cellar. As a result of his efforts, the restaurant has won the *Best of Award of Excellence* from the *Wine Spectator* for every year since 1987.

Best of Award of Excellence

Lobster Au Gratin

appetizer

Ingredients

1½ cups shiitake or button mushrooms
2 tablespoons shallots, minced
1¾ cups lobster meat, rough chopped
½ cup sherry wine
¼ cup cream
1 ounce butter
1 teaspoon parsley, chopped
¾ cup Gruyere, grated
¼ cup Parmesan, grated
¼ cup breadcrumbs, fine grind
salt and pepper to taste

Preparation

HEAT oven to broil. Sauté the mushrooms and shallots until the shallots are opaque. Add the lobster meat and cook for 30 seconds. Deglaze the pan with sherry, and reduce by half. Add cream, butter, and parsley, and reduce by half. Transfer to a small casserole dish (depth of the mix must be ½ inch) and top with Gruyere, then Parmesan, and then the breadcrumbs. Finish in the oven until golden brown.

Serves 4

Wine suggestion: Merry Edwards Sauvignon Blanc 2003

Sizzle Salad

This salad is very good as an entrée when you add your favorite meat.

Ingredients

- 4 *tablespoons garlic, minced*
- 4 *tablespoons shallots, minced*
- ¼ *cup white wine*
- 3 *tablespoons balsamic vinegar*
- ½ *cup chicken stock or broth*
- 2 *tablespoons sambal oelek, or as desired*
- 4 *cups penne, cooked al dente*
- 4 *ounces butter, in small cubes*
- ¾ *pound mixed greens (spring mix)*
- *salt to taste*

Preparation

SAUTÉ the garlic and shallots until golden, deglaze with white wine, and reduce until au sec (almost dry). Add the balsamic vinegar, chicken stock, sambal oelek, and penne. Reduce heat to half and add the butter slowly. Stir until fully incorporated. Toss with the mixed greens and serve

Serves 4

Wine suggestion: Pinot Gris Reserve Personelle 2000 by Trimbach

KUROBUTA PORK CHOPS

with Apple Vanilla Rum Sauce and Roasted Pine Nut Risotto

Ingredients

- *4 Kurobuta pork chops*
- *2 tablespoons ground cinnamon*
- *2 tablespoons all purpose flour*
- *Apple Vanilla Rum Sauce (recipe follows)*
- *Roasted Pine Nut Risotto (recipe follows)*

Preparation

HEAT oven to 400 degrees. Blend the cinnamon and flour together. Dredge pork chops in the mix and pan sear on both sides. Finish in the oven until desired temperature is reached. Medium is recommended.

Serves 4

Beverage Suggestions: Russian Hill Meredith Vineyard Pinot Noir, Dutton Goldfield Rued Vineyard Chardonnay, or Guinness Stout

For the Apple Vanilla Rum Sauce

- *2 apples*
- *1 tablespoon shallots, minced*
- *1 vanilla bean, cut in half*
- *1 cup dark rum (Brugal)*
- *16 ounces beef stock*
- *4 ounces cold butter, cut in chunks*

PEEL, core, and grate the apples. Sauté the shallots for 10 seconds, add apples and cook for 30 seconds, and then add rum. After the alcohol has burned off, add vanilla bean and beef stock, and reduce by half. Finish by mixing in the butter a few chunks at a time.

For the Roasted Pine Nut Risotto

- *2 tablespoons shallots, minced*
- *½ cup Arborio rice*
- *1½ cups vegetable stock, chicken stock, or water*
- *½ cup pine nuts, roasted*

SAUTÉ the shallots and rice for 2 minutes, stirring constantly. Add ½ cup of stock (or water). When absorbed, add second ½ cup, and so forth until all liquid has been added and absorbed. Stir in the roasted pine nuts.

Toasted Coconut Cheesecake

with Mango Lime Sauce

Ingredients

- 1½ *cups flour*
- 1 *cup sugar, divided*
- ¼ *pound butter*
- 1 *pound cream cheese, room temperature*
- ¼ *cup sour cream*
- ½ *tablespoon pure vanilla*
- ¾ *cup coconut milk*
- 1 *cup toasted coconut*
- 8 *eggs*
- *powdered sugar, for garnish*
- *Mango Lime Sauce (recipe follows)*
- *natural coconut curls, for garnish*

Preparation

HEAT oven to 325 degrees. In a food processor, mix the flour, ½ cup of the sugar, and butter until a coarse meal is formed. Press into a six-inch springform pan that has been well buttered and wrapped in aluminum foil. Bake until lightly browned, and then cool.

USING a mixer with a paddle attachment, mix the cream cheese and the remaining ½ cup sugar until smooth and creamy, scraping down the sides of the bowl frequently. Add sour cream and then vanilla, coconut milk, and toasted coconut. Mix until smooth and add eggs until just combined. Pour the batter into the cooled springform pan. Bake in a water bath at 325 degrees for approximately 1 hour. Cool in a water bath for 30 minutes. Remove from the water bath and refrigerate overnight.

TO SERVE, remove the cheesecake from the pan and dust with powdered sugar. Cut into serving portions. Pool Mango Lime Sauce on plates, place slices of cheesecake on top, and garnish with natural coconut curls. Enjoy!

Serves 6

Wine suggestion: Enkircher Batterieberg Vineyard Spätlese Riesling 2003

For the Mango Lime Sauce

- 2 *cups mangos, diced*
- ½ *cup water*
- ⅓ *cup sugar*
- 1 *lime, juice and zest from*

IN A saucepan, add the mangos, water, sugar, limejuice, and lime zest, and cook over a low heat until the mangos dissolve. Process in a food processor until smooth and adjust the seasoning if needed. Chill until served.

Cottonwood Grill

701 Yampa Avenue
Steamboat Springs, CO 80477
970-789-2229
www.cottonwoodgrill.com

Dinner – High Season:
5:00 to 10:00pm
Low Season: 5:30 to 9:00pm
Reservations appreciated

Cottonwood Grill

Peter Lautner and Michael Fragola, Chef/Owners

The Cottonwood Grill is a terrific reason to visit Steamboat Springs in the summer as well as the winter. Enjoy the crisp mountain air on a warm summer night on the circular wrap-around porch that overlooks the lush green yard and gardens, or take a table under the cottonwood trees, right beside the softly flowing Yampa River. Sitting under umbrellas, surrounded by hanging flower baskets and lanterns, enjoy a fine dining experience at the end of a busy day. Dining indoors is also a delight. Continuing the circular flow of the porch, large windows look outside on to the same scene. The light salmon-colored walls and wood trim set off the spectacular semi-circular cherry wood bar and the candlelit tables clothed in linen.

Chefs Peter Lautner and Michael Fragola teamed up to open the restaurant in December 2000. Peter graduated from the Culinary Institute of America and continued his professional training in New York City at Club 101, where he was appointed Executive Chef in 1989. Before opening Cottonwood Grill, he served as Executive Chef for Reebok International Headquarters in Boston. Originally from New York, Michael Fragola honed his culinary skills while practicing in Steamboat Springs and interning with many nationally recognized chefs. He garnered much recognition for his talents as the former Executive Chef of La Montana, a regionally and nationally published southwestern restaurant.

The chefs describe their cuisine as Pacific Rim, incorporating ingredients indigenous to the countries bordering the Pacific Ocean, with a considerable influence from Southeast Asia. In their words, "We begin with our roots, the delights from the American regions. We use the complex spices and exotic tastes from the east, the earthy chilies of Mexico, tender meats of Australia and New Zealand, and the wonderful array of seafood offered to us from the Pacific. We marry all these flavors together in a unique presentation of our cuisine." Their philosophy has proven to be a success, garnering them accolades in magazines such as *Food & Wine*, *Bon Appetite*, and *5280*. Most recently, they have received the *Wine Spectator's Award of Excellence* for their superb wine list.

Award of Excellence

Cottonwood Shrimp and Crab Cakes

with Wasabi Aioli

Ingredients

- 1¼ cup shrimp, cleaned and dry
- 1¼ cup cooked Canadian snow crab
- ½ cup water chestnuts, chopped
- ½ teaspoon garlic, minced
- 1 teaspoon salt and white pepper mix
- 1½ teaspoons cilantro, minced
- 1 tablespoon red bell pepper, brunoise
- 1 egg
- 1½ tablespoons flour
- 3 tablespoons breadcrumbs
- olive oil for sautéing
- dressed field greens
- Wasabi Aioli (recipe follows)

Preparation

PULSE shrimp in food processor until minced. Drain moisture from crab until mostly dry, pick clean, and mix with the shrimp. Mix water chestnuts, garlic, salt and pepper, cilantro, bell pepper, egg, flour, and breadcrumbs into shrimp and crab mix. Sauté a small piece for a taste test. Adjust seasonings if needed. Form mixture into 2-½ ounce cakes and let sit for 2 hours.

HEAT oven to 400 degrees. Sauté cakes in olive oil, and then finish in the oven for 8 – 10 minutes. Serve over dressed field greens and finish with the Wasabi Aioli.

Yield 8 cakes

For the Wasabi Aioli

- 1 cup mayonnaise
- 1½ teaspoons garlic, roasted
- 3 tablespoons water
- 1½ teaspoons lemon juice
- ⅛ teaspoon salt
- 1 tablespoon wasabi

MIX mayonnaise, garlic, water, lemon juice, salt, and wasabi in a stainless steel bowl. Hold for 24 hours. Strain through strainer and serve.

Sake-Lime Marinated Chilean Sea Bass

with Green Curry Coconut Soba Noodles

Ingredients

- 3 cups mirin
- 1 cup sake
- 1½ limes, juiced
- 2 pounds Chilean sea bass
- Green Curry Coconut Soba Noodles (recipe follows)

Preparation

MIX mirin, sake, and limejuice for a marinade. Trim the fish and marinate for 24 hours.

HEAT oven to 400 degrees. Sear the fish in a hot sauté pan, and then finish in the oven for 11 to 15 minutes, depending on desired doneness. Serve over Green Curry Coconut Soba Noodles and your choice of vegetables.

Serves 4

For the Green Curry Coconut Soba Noodles

- 24 ounces coconut milk
- 2 tablespoons green curry paste
- 1½ teaspoons fish sauce
- salt and pepper to taste
- 1 pound soba noodles, cooked

REDUCE coconut milk by half. Add green curry paste, fish sauce, and salt and pepper. Simmer 5 minutes; add warmed noodles to the sauce. Toss and simmer until desired consistency is reached. Do not overcook noodles.

Hoisin Ginger Marinated Pork Tenderloin

with a Cilantro Curry Sauce

Ingredients

- 1 *cup Hoisin sauce*
- 1 *cup water*
- 1¼ *teaspoon garlic, minced*
- 1½ *teaspoon ginger, minced*
- ¼ *cup sesame oil*
- ¾ *teaspoon fish sauce*
- 1 ½ *pounds pork tenderloin, trimmed*
- *Cilantro Curry Sauce (recipe follows)*

Preparation

MIX the Hoisin sauce, water, garlic, ginger, sesame oil, and fish sauce to make a marinade. Marinate the pork for 24 hours.

HEAT oven to 400 degrees. Sear pork in hot pan, and finish in the oven until it reaches an internal temperature of 145 degrees. Slice and serve with the Cilantro Curry Sauce. Vegetable fried rice makes an excellent accompaniment to this dish.

Serves 4

For the Cilantro Curry Sauce

- 1½ *teaspoons shallot, minced*
- ¾ *teaspoon garlic, minced*
- 3 *tablespoons butter*
- 3 *tablespoons flour*
- 1 *cup demi-glace*
- 1 *cup chicken broth*
- 1½ *teaspoons green curry paste*
- 3 *tablespoons cilantro*
- *salt and pepper to taste*

SAUTÉ the shallot and garlic in butter. Add the flour, stir, and cook while stirring until slightly brown, 5-7 minutes. Do not burn. Add demi-glace and chicken broth. Bring to a boil and add green curry paste. Simmer 15 minutes, then strain. Add the cilantro and blend in a blender. Do not strain. You can adjust consistency by adding water to thin, or reduce in a pan to thicken. Season with salt and pepper to taste.

Twice Roasted Chinese Five Spice Peking Duck

with Cherry Merlot Sauce

Ingredients

- *2 Peking ducks*
- *2 tablespoons sesame oil*
- *2 tablespoons salt and white pepper*
- *1 tablespoon Chinese 5-spice*
- *chicken stock for reheating*
- *Cherry Glaze (recipe follows)*
- *Cherry Merlot Sauce (recipe follows)*

Preparation

YOU may prepare the duck the day before. Defrost the ducks completely. Remove wings at the first joint. Reserve necks and wings for stock. Rub with sesame oil and season with salt and white pepper mix. Sprinkle Chinese 5-spice over duck evenly. Place ducks breast down in a roasting pan.

HEAT oven to 475 degrees. Roast ducks for 15 minutes, drain the fat, and roll duck breasts up. Reduce temperature to 275 degrees and roast ducks for 1-½ hours, rotating ducks every half hour. Remove ducks when their internal temperature reaches 154 degrees. Cool entirely.

WHEN cool, butcher the ducks in half. Bone and follow along the rib cage and thighbone. Keep bones for duck stock. Remove upper thighbone by making incisions along each side and underneath, twist and remove. Cut each half duck in between the thigh and the breast to form two pieces.

ON THE DAY of the meal, re-heat the ducks at 400 degrees on a pan with some chicken stock for 12 – 15 minutes. Brush with the Cherry Glaze, and slice the breast and thigh for presentation. Finish with the Cherry Merlot Sauce, and starch and vegetable of your choice.

Serves 4

For the Cherry Glaze

- *¼ cup dried tart cherries*
- *¾ teaspoon ginger, minced*
- *1½ tablespoons sugar*
- *2 teaspoons plum sauce*
- *1¼ cups water, divided*
- *1 tablespoon cornstarch*
- *salt and pepper to taste*

MIX the cherries, ginger, sugar, plum sauce, and 1 cup of the water together and bring to a boil. Lower heat and simmer for 15 minutes. Purée in a blender and return to the pot. Mix the cornstarch and remaining ¼ cup water and add to the puréed glaze. Simmer for 10 minutes, strain, and cool. You may adjust the consistency with the addition of cornstarch slurry or water. Season to taste with salt and pepper.

For the Cherry Merlot Sauce

- 1½ *teaspoons shallots, minced*
- ½ *teaspoon oil*
- 8 *ounces merlot, fruit forward*
- ¾ *cups dried tart cherries*
- 1 *quart duck stock or chicken broth*
- 2 *teaspoons honey*
- 2 *tablespoons butter*
- 2 *tablespoons flour*
- *salt and pepper to taste*

SWEAT the shallots in oil. Deglaze with the red wine, add the cherries and reduce by half. Add the stock and honey and reduce by ⅔. Make a roux with the butter and flour, and cook for 5 minutes. Temper hot sauce into roux until smooth, add back to the sauce, and simmer for 15 minutes. Add water to loosen the consistency, or reduce to thicken. Season to taste.

A horse-drawn sleigh leaves a trail in the snow near Leadville circa 1925.

Ranch House Restaurant
Devil's Thumb Ranch
3530 County Road 83
Tabernash, CO
970-726-5632
www.devilsthumbranch.com
Summer Hours:
early June – early October
Winter Hours:
late November – early April
Call for hours

Ranch House Restaurant

Trish Cyman, Executive Chef

The romantic Ranch House Restaurant is located at Devils Thumb Ranch, a spectacular 4,000-acre property that has been turned into an intimate resort with a decidedly western flavor. The resort offers an abundance of winter sports and summer sports, including a fully stocked flyfishing shop and award winning cross-country ski center on premises. Lodging is provided in cozy cabins, and a luxurious spa and outdoor pool add to the fun.

The saloon and restaurant are housed in the original circa 1937 log homestead. Vaulted ceilings and thick wooden beams in the saloon and lounge area top the polished log walls. On winter weekends, you can expect to find a musician strumming his guitar and singing western tunes. A wide wrap around enclosed porch has been added to the structure to serve as the main dining room. The numerous picture windows look out to a beautiful meadow and unobstructed view of the Continental Divide. For special parties, the intimate wine cellar is the perfect place for a celebration. The cellar is well stocked with a wide variety of vintages. The beautiful cherry wine racks and beams were crafted from 150-year-old cherry trees harvested on the owner's family land in Adirondack Park, New York.

The Ranch House Restaurant lives up to the natural beauty of this ranch. Executive Chef, Trish Cyman, has insisted on a culinary philosophy for the restaurant that stresses fresh and organic, whenever possible. Seafood is flown in fresh, and the beef and pork is purchased from the Niman Ranch, a high-end supplier of humanely raised organic meats. Much of the produce is grown locally and organically. All desserts, sauces, and salads are homemade from scratch. This emphasis on fresh and healthy foods shows in the quality of the finished dishes that are presented to diners.

Whether staying at the ranch or just visiting, you will find a warm and friendly atmosphere that will pull you in to the western experience and offer you a wonderful array of succulent dishes prepared and served with care.

Hot Portabella Mushroom Salad

with Passion Fruit Vinaigrette

Ingredients

- ¾ cup olive oil
- ¼ cup red wine vinegar
- ¼ cup balsamic vinegar
- 2 garlic cloves, minced
- 1 bay leaf
- 10 peppercorns
- ½ teaspoon dry mustard
- 1 pinch sugar
- 4 portabella mushroom caps, without the stems
- 8 ounces fresh goat cheese, lightly whipped
- 8 ounces mixed organic greens of choice
- 4 ounces, Passion Fruit Vinaigrette (recipe follows)
- white truffle oil to drizzle

Preparation

HEAT oven to 350 degrees. Combine the olive oil, vinegars, garlic, bay leaf, peppercorns, mustard, and sugar. Heat this marinade and boil for 5 minutes. Blanch the mushroom caps in the marinade for 1 minute, then drain. When cool, fill the caps with goat cheese. Bake for 5 minutes or until hot.

TO SERVE, toss the salad greens in the Passion Fruit Vinaigrette. Place the mushroom caps on top and drizzle with truffle oil.

Serves 4

For the Passion Fruit Vinaigrette

- 1 cup passion fruit purée
- 1 cup rice wine vinegar
- 3 tablespoons orange juice
- 3 tablespoons lime juice
- 3 tablespoons lemon juice
- ½ cup canola oil
- ½ cup peanut oil (if it is strongly flavored, use less of it and more canola
- 2 tablespoons cilantro, chopped
- 2 tablespoons shallot, minced
- 2 tablespoons red bell pepper, minced
- salt and honey to taste

COMBINE the passion fruit purée, vinegar, orange juice, lime juice, and lemon juice. Slowly add the canola and peanut oil to create an emulsion. Then add the cilantro, shallot, bell pepper, and salt and honey.

Ratatouille over Polenta

Ingredients

- *1 eggplant (about 1 pound)*
- *1 teaspoon salt*
- *2 tablespoons olive oil*
- *1 cup onion, chopped*
- *1 teaspoon garlic, minced*
- *1 pound summer squash, sliced*
- *½ cup red bell pepper, chopped*
- *3 tomatoes, roasted, peeled, and chopped*
- *3 tablespoons fresh basil, finely chopped*
- *1 teaspoon dry oregano*
- *salt and pepper to taste*
- *thin shavings of Parmesan Reggiano, to garnish*
- *1 ounce prosciutto or speck, thinly sliced*
- *½ tablespoon balsamic glaze*
- *½ tablespoon basil oil*
- *Polenta (recipe follows)*

Preparation

CUT the eggplant into 1-inch cubes and sprinkle with the salt. Let it sit in a colander for 1 hour. Rinse, drain, and pat dry.

HEAT the olive oil in a large skillet. Add the onions and cook until soft. Add the garlic, eggplant, squash, and red pepper. Sauté until soft. Add the tomatoes, basil, oregano, and salt and pepper to taste. Cook until the vegetables have softened and come together.

TO SERVE, pour the Ratatouille over the Polenta. Top with the prosciutto and the Parmesan. Garnish with basil oil and balsamic glaze.

Serves 4

For the Polenta

- *2½ cups water*
- *3 cups milk*
- *3 teaspoons salt*
- *1 pound coarse-grained yellow cornmeal (known in stores as polenta)*

COMBINE the water, milk, and salt in a heavy bottomed saucepan or pot. Bring to a steady boil. Pour a fistful of cornmeal in a thin stream into the boiling liquid, stirring with a whisk. Slowly add the remainder of the cornmeal, whisking all the time. Lower the heat and stir with a wooden spoon for up to 40 minutes, or until the polenta pulls away from the sides of the pot.

Trout with Warm Tomato Salsa

Ingredients

- ⅓ *cup cornmeal*
- ½ *cup flour*
- 1 *tablespoon Chimayo medium chili powder*
- 1 *pinch salt and pepper*
- 4 *whole trout, skin-on, boned, and scaled*
- 6 *tablespoons frying oil*
- *toasted pumpkin seeds to garnish*
- *Warm Tomato Salsa (recipe follows)*

Preparation

HEAT the oven to 350 degrees. Mix the cornmeal, flour, chili powder, and salt and pepper in a dish. Dip the trout in the mixture to coat. Sauté the coated trout in the hot oil. Flip, and sauté the other side. Finish in the oven. Top with the Warm Tomato Salsa and garnish with toasted pumpkin seeds.

Serves 4

For the Warm Tomato Salsa

- 2 *tablespoons butter*
- 1 *teaspoon shallots, minced*
- 1 *teaspoon Serrano chili pepper, minced*
- 1 *teaspoon garlic*
- 6 *grape or cherry tomatoes, halved or quartered*
- 2 *cups Sauvignon Blanc wine*
- 1 *tablespoon agave nectar*
- ¼ *cup fish stock (optional)*
- 1 *tablespoon cilantro, chopped*

IN THE butter, sauté the shallots, Serrano pepper, and garlic. Add the tomatoes and sauté briefly in the hot skillet. Pour the wine in the pan. Add the agave nectar and reduce by half. If using, add the fish stock. Reduce until most of the liquid has become slightly thick. Add the cilantro and reserve until serving.

Grilled Pork Chops with Berry Salsa

Ingredients

4 bone-in Niman Ranch pork chops
1 tablespoon oil
salt and pepper to taste
Berry Salsa (recipe follows)

Preparation

RUB the oil over the pork chops and season with salt and pepper. Grill the pork chops over moderate heat to desired temperature. Top with the Berry Salsa.

Serves 4

For the Berry Salsa

2 pints fresh blackberries
½ pint strawberries, diced
1 pint fresh raspberries, diced
2 shallots, minced
½ teaspoon fresh ginger, grated
3 cloves garlic, minced
2-5 jalapeno peppers, minced
2 serrano peppers, minced
3 limes, juice and zest from
roasted sesame oil to taste (a good ratio is one part sesame to 3 parts lime juice)
1 bunch cilantro, minced (about ¼ cup) or to taste
salt and pepper to taste

COMBINE the berries, shallots, ginger, garlic, peppers, lime juice and zest, sesame oil, and cilantro. Season with salt and pepper to taste, and reserve for serving.

Slow Roasted Niman Ranch Tenderloin
with Horseradish Cream Sauce

Ingredients

- 2 *teaspoons oil*
- ½ *teaspoon kosher salt*
- 2 *teaspoons coarse black pepper*
- 2 *teaspoons garlic, minced*
- 1 *whole tenderloin, cleaned of silver skin and with the chain removed*
- 10 *sprigs rosemary*
- 10 *sprigs oregano*
- 10 *sprigs thyme*
- *Horseradish Cream Sauce (recipe follows)*

Preparation

HEAT the oven to 250 degrees. Mix the oil, salt, pepper, and garlic, together. Rub the tenderloin with this mix and let it come to room temperature. Place in the oven in a shallow roasting pan over the fresh herbs for 20-30 minutes, or until the desired internal temperature is reached (rare is 120-125, medium rare is 125-130, medium is 130-135, and anything after that is a waste of Niman Ranch beef!). Raise the heat to 425 degrees and finish for 5-10 minutes. Remove from the oven and let rest for 5-10 minutes.

TO SERVE, slice the tenderloin to the desired thickness and serve with the Horseradish Cream Sauce.

Serves 4

For the Horseradish Cream Sauce

- 2 *cups sour cream or crème fraîche*
- ¼ *cup prepared horseradish (or to taste)*
- *salt and pepper to taste*

COMBINE the sour cream or crème fraîche, horseradish, and salt and pepper. Reserve for serving.

Grilled Antelope with Prickly Pear Sauce

Ingredients

- *4 6-ounce boneless leg filets of antelope*
- *salt and pepper*
- *oil*
- *nopalitos (chopped prickly pear pads) for garnish*
- *Prickly Pear Sauce (recipe follows)*

Preparation

COAT the antelope with the oil and salt and pepper. Grill to desired doneness and slice thinly. Plate the antelope with the sauce and garnish with nopalitos.

Serves 4

For the Prickly Pear Sauce

- *¼ cup shallots, minced*
- *¼ cup garlic, minced*
- *2 ounces clarified butter*
- *2 cups tequila (preferably a good one)*
- *1-2 cups veal stock*
- *8 ounces prickly pear syrup*
- *4 ounces prickly pear nectar*

SAUTÉ the shallots and garlic in butter until soft. Add the tequila to the pan and reduce by half. In a separate pan, reduce the veal stock by half, and then add to the tequila mixture. Reduce by ¼. Stir in the prickly pear syrup and nectar until hot. If a smoother sauce is preferred, strain through a fine sieve.

Swiss Tart with Colorado Peaches

Ingredients

- 8 *ounces puff pastry*
- 3 *tablespoons walnuts or almonds, ground*
- 2 *pounds fresh peaches, sliced thinly*
- 5 *tablespoons sugar, divided*
- 1 *teaspoon vanilla*
- 3 *eggs*
- 1 *cup heavy cream*

Preparation

HEAT oven to 400 degrees. Roll out the puff pastry to fill the bottom of a tart pan. Cover the dough with the ground nuts. Then line the dough with sliced peaches. Sprinkle with 2 tablespoons of the sugar and bake for 20 minutes. Whisk the vanilla, eggs, cream, and the remaining sugar together and pour the mixture over the fruit. Bake for a further 15-20 minutes or until the custard is set.

Serves 8 - 10

The Wine Spectator Award

Many of the restaurants included in this cookbook have been recognized by Wine Spectator, the world's most popular wine magazine. It reviews more than 10,000 wines each year and covers travel, fine dining and the lifestyle of wine for novices and connoisseurs alike. Through its Restaurant Awards program, the magazine recognizes restaurants around the world that offer distinguished wine lists.

Awards are given in three tiers. In 2003, more than 3,600 restaurants earned wine list awards. To qualify, wine lists must provide vintages and appellations for all selections. The overall presentation and appearance of the list are also important. Once past these initial requirements, lists are then judged for one of three awards: the Award of Excellence, the Best of Award of Excellence, and the Grand Award.

- Award of Excellence—The basic Award of Excellence recognizes restaurants with lists that offer a well-chosen selection of quality producers, along with a thematic match to the menu in both price and style.
- Best of Award of Excellence—The second-tier Best of Award of Excellence was created to give special recognition to those restaurants that exceed the requirements of the basic category. These lists must display vintage depth, including vertical offerings of several top wines, as well as excellent breadth from major wine growing regions.
- Grand Award—The highest award, the Grand Award, is given to those restaurants that show an uncompromising, passionate devotion to quality. These lists show serious depth of mature vintages, outstanding breadth in their vertical offerings, excellent harmony with the menu, and superior organization and presentation. In 2003, only 89 restaurants held Wine Spectator Grand Awards.

Award of Excellence

Best of Award of Excellence

Grand Award

Gasthaus Eichler

78786 US Hwy 40
Winter Park, CO
www.gasthauseichler.com
970-726-5133

Dinner served nightly 5:00 – 9:00pm

Gasthaus Eichler

René Weder, Executive Chef/Owner
Joan Weder, Owner

A touch of the Swiss Alps will envelope you as you enter the cozy Gasthaus Eichler in Winter Park. René and Joan Weder will make sure that your stay, whether for an evening or for several days, is immersed in the tradition of European hospitality. Hans and Hannelore Eichler of the Rhein Valley, Germany custom built the inn in 1987 of white stucco and dark log. Fifteen comfortable rooms are available, all with views of the surrounding mountains or the creek that wanders through the property. As a bed and breakfast, guests are treated to a European breakfast in The Lounge. Lunch is also served there during the spring, summer, and fall. But the sumptuous dinner fare in Dezéley's is the crowning glory after a day spent in the fresh Colorado mountain air.

The Weders purchased the inn from the Eichler's in 2003. René Weder, originally from Rhein Valley, Switzerland, received his formal culinary training in Europe and came to America in 1984. He has worked for such notable establishments as the Boca Raton Hotel & Resort, the Beaver Creek Hyatt, as well as serving as the Executive Chef at the Brown Palace Hotel in Denver. It was at the Brown Palace that he interviewed a young woman from Sleepy Hollow, New York for a job. Joan had spent twelve years working for the Nestle-Stouffer firm and had fallen in love with Colorado in 1993 on a visit. Love bloomed, and the couple were married a couple of years later. Shortly after their marriage, the Weders moved to Georgia, where René took the position of Food & Beverage Director for the Chateau Élan Hotels and Resorts. But they continued to hold a special place in their hearts for the mountains of Colorado. This attraction led them to start a new life for themselves with the purchase of the inn and its dining rooms.

Dézeley's provides Continental cuisine in a lovely dining room overlooking Vasquez Creek and the Arapahoe National Forest. Live piano music adds a special touch to dinners on Friday and Sunday evenings. The Fondue Stube, a cozy bar area with a large stone fireplace, is the perfect place to warm up at après ski. Fondue is served nightly in the winter months and is served for special parties of ten or more throughout the rest of the year.

Smoked Salmon Tartare

Unlike the well-known Beef Tartare, this dish consists of fully cooked ingredients.

Ingredients

- 16 *ounces smoked salmon, sliced*
- 3 *tablespoons sour cream*
- 1 *tablespoon mayonnaise*
- ¼ *teaspoon capers, rinsed and chopped*
- ¼ *teaspoon Dijon mustard*
- 1 *teaspoon red onion, chopped*
- ½ *teaspoon parsley, chopped*
- ½ *lemon, juice from*
- 1 *teaspoon vodka*
- *salt and pepper to taste*
- *toasted bread, crackers, or vegetable crudités, as accompaniment*

Preparation

MIX the sour cream, mayonnaise, capers, mustard, onion, parsley, lemon juice, and vodka in a bowl, and season to taste. Finely chop the smoked salmon and add to the mixture. Form salmon into even shaped servings or place in a decorative bowl and serve with toasted bread, crackers, or crudités vegetables.

Serves 4

Wine Suggestion: Rodney Strong Chardonnay

Spätzle

Spätzle is a dish of tiny noodles or dumplings and is served as a side dish, much like potatoes or rice. It is often accompanied by a sauce or gravy.

Ingredients

- *½ pound flour*
- *½ teaspoon salt*
- *1 pinch nutmeg*
- *¾ cup milk*
- *2 eggs*
- *salt to taste*
- *butter to taste*

Preparation

SIFT flour, salt, and nutmeg into a mixing bowl. Form a well in the center of this mixture. Combine lukewarm milk with eggs, and pour into well. Gradually stir in the flour with a wooden spoon until dough takes on a thick consistency. Beat dough until bubbles start to form. Force dough through a sieve or colander with large holes, directly into boiling salted water. Once spätzle floats to the top, remove immediately and rinse under cool water. Sauté lightly in butter and serve. Spätzle dough can be seasoned with saffron, chopped spinach, tomato purée, or poppy seeds.

Serves 4 – 5 as a side dish

Veal Saltimbocca

This is a Roman specialty which, when translated, means "jump mouth."

Ingredients

- *1¼ pounds veal cutlets*
- *8 sage leaves*
- *2 ounces prosciutto*
- *salt and pepper to taste*
- *1 ounce flour*
- *2 ounces butter*
- *½ cup Marsala wine*
- *1 cup veal stock*

Preparation

SLICE veal cutlets thinly into eight slices and place a sage leaf and a slice of prosciutto on each cutlet, securing with a toothpick. Season with salt and pepper, dredge the cutlets in flour, and sauté them in butter until golden brown. Deglaze the pan with Marsala and veal stock and simmer for 2 minutes. Remove the toothpick and arrange the cutlets on a platter or individual plates. Place half the sauce over the veal and serve the remaining sauce on the side.

Serves 4

Wine suggestion: Dr. Loosen Riesling Spatlese

Apple Strudel

This is a traditional Central European dessert.

Ingredients

4 red delicious apples
½ cup sugar
2 teaspoons cinnamon
2 ounces raisins
12-14 ounces puff pastry sheet
1 ounce bread crumbs
1 ounce sliced almonds
1 egg
powdered sugar
vanilla bean ice cream

Preparation

HEAT the oven to 375 degrees. Peel, core, and slice apples and place in a mixing bowl. Add the sugar, cinnamon, and raisins. Unfold the pastry sheet and place on a greased cookie sheet. Sprinkle breadcrumbs and sliced almonds on the lower half of the dough. Beat the egg and brush a thin layer on the upper half of the dough. Place the apple mixture on top of the almonds and breadcrumbs and roll up the puff pastry around the filling. Press the dough together along the two ends. Brush with remaining egg and bake in the oven at 375 degrees for 30 to 40 minutes. Strudel should be golden brown when done.

STRUDEL is best when served warm. Cut it into slices, top with powdered sugar, and serve with a scoop of vanilla bean ice cream.

Serves 4 – 6

Wine suggestion: Late Harvest Semillon

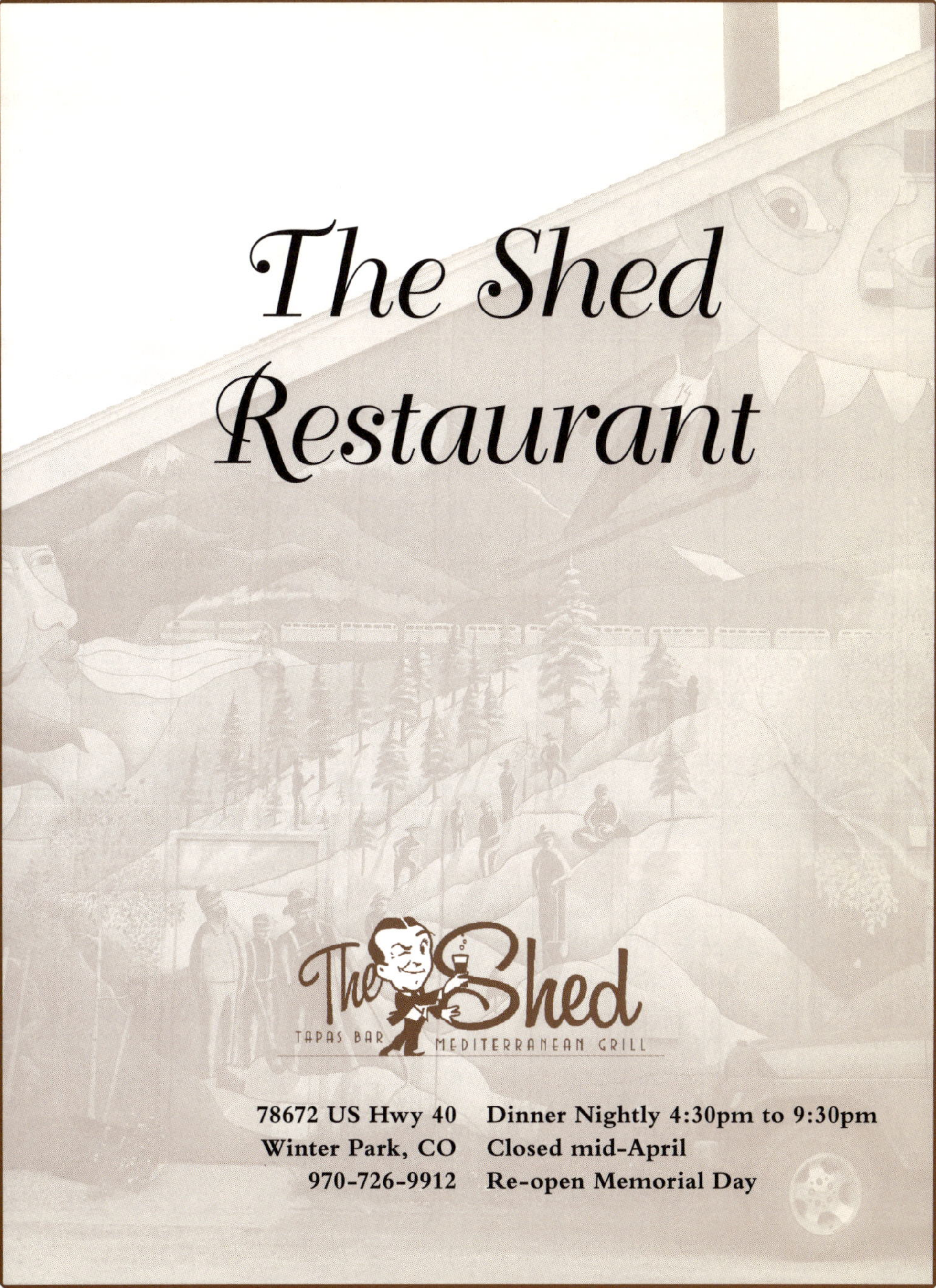

The Shed Restaurant

The Shed
TAPAS BAR MEDITERRANEAN GRILL

78672 US Hwy 40
Winter Park, CO
970-726-9912

Dinner Nightly 4:30pm to 9:30pm
Closed mid-April
Re-open Memorial Day

The Shed Restaurant

Ted & Jess Kutrumbos, Owners

The Shed Restaurant had a significant makeover when its new owners took over in June 2005. This funky little place had been a southwestern restaurant for nearly nine years, but Ted and Jess had other plans for it. With their strong background in Mediterranean cuisine, they offer a wide variety of fresh and delicious tapas, salads, and entrées that delight the locals and the tourists alike.

Ted Kutrumbos has the restaurant business in his blood. His father, Deno, grew up working in his parents' restaurants on the Jersey shore. Ted's parents moved to Winter Park in 1973 and Ted remembers helping out at The Swiss House, where his father was chef at the time. He was just six years old and could barely see over the tables. Later, his father bought The Swiss House and turned it into Deno's Mountain Bistro that he still owns today. Ted and Jess met in Boulder while working at Jess' godparents' Italian restaurant, Laudisio. Being two children of restaurant families, they naturally hit it off and have been together ever since.

As you walk into The Shed, you can turn left into the colorful bar area with a fireplace and seating at the bar or at high tables with stools. It's the perfect place to enjoy a sociable evening with a few libations and a sampling of the delicious tapas. The multi-level interior dining areas feature colorful walls adorned with paintings of Mediterranean scenes. Dinner is served on simple wooden tables befitting a ski town, and festive Italian lights are strung from the wood beams throughout the building. Ted and the kitchen staff have put together a mouth-watering menu featuring a tour of the Mediterranean. Diners can select from entrées such as halibut with goat cheese and fig orzo, pork scaloppini with lemon, capers and cherry tomatoes, or tuna ceviche with tzatsiki. The Shed is the only restaurant in Winter Park where you can get such Mediterranean staples as hummus, falafel, and saganaki. And for those steak lovers, try a grilled ribeye with Cabrales bleu cheese.

In the summer, there's nothing like sitting out on the patio enjoying a spectacular sunset over the Rockies, while sipping on a pitcher of sangria while munching on mussels provençal, marinated olives, and a selection of tapas.

Insalata Panzanella
with Rosemary Lemon Vinaigrette

Ingredients

- 8-10 *slices day-old crusty bread, cut into 1-inch cubes*
- ½ *pound mixed field greens*
- 1 *tablespoon fresh basil, coarsely chopped*
- 1 *tablespoon fresh dill, coarsely chopped*
- 1 *tablespoon fresh Italian parsley, coarsely chopped*
- 1 *tablespoon fresh tarragon, coarsely chopped*
- 1½ *cups cherry tomatoes, halved*
- 1 *cup mixed nuts, chopped*
- ½ *cup pecorino Romano cheese, grated*
- 1 *cup dried figs, sliced*
- *Rosemary Lemon Vinaigrette (recipe follows)*

Preparation

WARM the bread slightly. Combine greens, basil, dill, Italian parsley, tarragon, tomatoes, nuts, cheese, and figs in a mixing bowl and toss lightly to combine. Toss with the Rosemary Lemon Vinaigrette and serve.

Serves 4 as an entrée or 6–8 side salads

For the Rosemary Lemon Vinaigrette

- ½ *cup champagne vinegar*
- ¼ *cup fresh lemon juice*
- 1 *lemon, zest from*
- 2 *tablespoons fresh rosemary*
- ¼ *cup honey*
- 1 *teaspoon salt*
- 1 *pinch white pepper*
- 1 *teaspoon shallots, minced*
- 1 *tablespoon Dijon mustard*
- 2 *cups canola oil*

COMBINE vinegar, lemon juice and zest, rosemary, honey, salt, pepper, shallots, and mustard in a blender or food processor. With machine running, add oil in a thin stream until it is all incorporated. Adjust the seasoning to taste.

Pan Seared Halibut

with Tarragon Beurre Blanc and Goat Cheese-Fig Orzo

Ingredients

- 6 *6-ounce halibut filets*
- *salt and pepper to taste*
- *oil to sauté*
- *Tarragon Beurre Blanc (recipe follows)*
- *Goat Cheese-Fig Orzo (recipe follows)*
- 6 *tablespoons toasted almonds for garnish*

Preparation

SEASON the filets with a little salt and pepper. In a nonstick pan over medium heat, sauté the halibut in a little oil, turning only after the fish has turned a golden brown on the cooking side (4-5 minutes). After turning, cook for another 5 minutes. Keep warm on a heated platter.

TO SERVE, place the Goat Cheese-Fig Orzo in the center of each plate, top with a vegetable of your choice, such as steamed asparagus, and then top with the fish. Spoon the Tarragon Beurre Blanc sauce over the fish and garnish with toasted almonds.

Serves 6

For the Tarragon Beurre Blanc

- ½ *cup Madeira*
- 1 *teaspoon garlic, minced*
- ½ *teaspoon shallot, minced*
- ¼ *cup tomato, diced*
- 2 *tablespoons heavy cream*
- ½ *teaspoon salt*
- ¼ *teaspoon pepper*
- 6 *ounces unsalted butter, cubed*
- 1 *teaspoon fresh tarragon, chopped*

OVER high heat, reduce the wine with the garlic, shallots, and tomatoes until the wine is almost gone. Add cream, salt, and pepper, and bring to a boil. Reduce heat to low and add butter, 1 cube at a time, stirring constantly until butter is all melted. Repeat until all the butter is added. Pour the sauce through a strainer over the tarragon, pressing on the solids. Stir sauce and adjust seasoning to taste.

For the Goat Cheese-Fig Orzo

- 1 *tablespoon shallot, minced*
- 1 *teaspoon garlic, minced*
- *oil to sauté*
- ½ *cup dry white wine*
- 1 *cup heavy cream*
- 1½ *teaspoons salt*
- 1 *teaspoon pepper*
- ¼ *pound goat cheese*
- ½ *pound orzo pasta, cooked al dente*
- ¼ *cup fresh basil, chopped*
- ¼ *cup dried figs, chopped*

SAUTÉ shallot and garlic in a little oil until shallot is translucent. Add wine and reduce until mostly gone. Add the cream, salt, and pepper and bring to a simmer. Turn off the heat and whisk in the goat cheese until completely dissolved. Set aside. Coat orzo lightly with oil and add basil, figs, and goat cheese sauce, combining thoroughly. Adjust seasoning to taste.

Tuscan Stuffed Pork Loin

with Sage Madeira Cream and Sun-Dried Tomato and Pine Nut Pilaf

Ingredients

2 ounces cappacolla ham, sliced thin and coarsely chopped
2 ounces prosciutto, sliced thin and coarsely chopped
2 ounces provolone cheese, shredded
1 ounce Parmesan cheese, shredded
1 teaspoon fresh thyme, chopped
1 teaspoon pepper
6 6-ounce cuts of pork loin
aged balsamic vinegar to drizzle
Sage Madeira Cream (recipe follows)
Sun-Dried Tomato and Pine Nut Pilaf (recipe follows)

Preparation

HEAT oven to 400 degrees. Combine the ham, prosciutto, provolone, Parmesan, thyme, and pepper. Lay each piece of pork loin on a flat surface and, using a small knife, cut a pocket into the side of each piece, leaving just a ¼ inch of pork still connected. Stuff each piece of pork with stuffing and press down to flatten slightly. Roast the pork in the oven for 15 minutes, or until internal temperature of the pork reaches 160 degrees. Set aside and keep it warm.

TO SERVE, place the Sun-Dried Tomato and Pine Nut Pilaf on a plate and top with the pork Spoon the Sage Madeira Cream over the pork and drizzle it with aged balsamic vinegar. Serve with a vegetable of your choice.

Serves 6

For the Sage Madeira Cream

1 tablespoon shallots, minced
1 tablespoon garlic, minced
oil to sauté
1 cup Madeira wine
1½ cups chicken stock
1½ cups heavy cream
1 tablespoon fresh sage, chopped
salt and pepper to taste
2 tablespoons cornstarch
2 tablespoons water

Tuscan Stuffed Pork Loin, continued

SAUTÉ the shallots and garlic in a little oil until translucent. Add the Madeira and reduce until it is almost gone. Add the stock and cream and bring to a simmer. Add the sage and salt and pepper and simmer for 5 minutes. Mix the cornstarch and water thoroughly. Add the cornstarch mixture to the sauce and bring to a simmer. Check for desired thickness (sauce should just start to stick to the back of a spoon). If sauce is not thickening, add a little more cornstarch mixture. (Note: sauce will not fully thicken until it has come back to a boil.) Adjust the seasoning to taste and keep warm for serving.

For the Sun-Dried Tomato and Pine Nut Pilaf

2 cups chicken stock
1 cup long grain rice
2 tablespoons sun-dried tomatoes, chopped
1 tablespoon fresh basil, chopped
¼ cup pine nuts, toasted
salt and pepper to taste

BRING the stock to a boil, add the rice, stir, reduce heat to medium-low and cover. Simmer the rice until liquid is almost gone. Remove from heat and let stand for 5 minutes. Fold the tomatoes, basil, and pine nuts into the rice. Adjust seasoning to taste.

Members of the Roundup Riders of the Rockies on horseback inside the Teller House Bar

Champeaux
Champeaux
Keystone Lodge
Keystone Village, CO
800-469-6130
Open nightly from 5:30 to 9:00pm
Reservations recommended

Champeaux

Scott Radek, Executive Chef

The only a la carte fine dining experience in the Keystone Resort complex, Champeaux features an excellent continental menu with a superb wine list that has been awarded the *Award of Excellence* by *Wine Spectator* magazine.

To get to this elegant restaurant, descend the open staircase in the lobby of the lodge. The restaurant is an oasis of calm in a very lively resort. The interior is decorated with thick, rich fabrics that have a luxurious feel and soften the noise of a busy restaurant. If an intimate dinner is what you desire, one of the secluded banquettes will be just what you want.

Executive Chef Scott Radek describes his love of the creative aspect of his career, "Food inspires me, how you coordinate basic elements to surprise and delight your guests… I want to give people a memorable meal, whether it's a special occasion or not, one that they will treasure in their thoughts later." Chef Radek's schooling came from thirteen years of heated kitchen experience. He worked as Executive Chef for Keystone Lodge in the early 90s, then as a seasonal chef in Bear Valley, California, and as Executive Chef of Pesce Fresco Restaurant at Copper Mountain. From there he moved to Taos, New Mexico to serve as Executive Chef at Doc Martin's Restaurant and also Chef de Cuisine at El Monte Sagrado Resort and Spa.

Returning to Keystone Lodge, Chef Radek also helps budding chefs garner on-the-job training experience through Colorado Mountain College's three-year Culinary Apprenticeship Program. He says of the program, "Two-thirds of my staff members are apprentices working full-time in the kitchen, while taking classes and doing their homework. When you graduate from CMC, you have what it takes to be a chef…it's not just theory."

Chef Radek's philosophy for Champeaux blends the fresh flavors indigenous to Colorado with Continental tastes, especially from France. He will often use cheeses from France, or the Jamon Serrano from Spain, but add Rocky Ford melons in season, or Olathe sweet corn during its harvest. Using a network of Colorado co-op farmers, he injects Colorado's seasonal flavors into whatever he is serving that night. When dining at Champeaux, be prepared to enjoy a special culinary experience.

Award of Excellence

Grilled Shrimp with Marinated Tomatoes

Ingredients

2 pounds roma tomatoes
6 anchovies, smashed
½ cup fresh basil, chopped
½ cup sherry vinegar
½ cup extra virgin olive oil
1 teaspoon kosher salt
½ teaspoon red chile flakes
4 cloves garlic, minced
1½ pounds large shrimp, peeled and deveined
olive oil to taste
salt and pepper to taste
1 baguette, sliced
lemon, sliced into wedges

Preparation

PEEL, seed, and chop the tomatoes. Combine tomatoes, anchovies, basil, sherry vinegar, olive oil, salt, red chili flakes, and garlic, and refrigerate overnight.

THREAD shrimp onto bamboo or metal skewers, drizzle with olive oil and season with salt and pepper. Slice baguette on bias and drizzle with olive oil.

IN SAUTÉ pan over charcoal fire, cook tomato mixture until bubbling and releasing perfume. Grill shrimp over charcoal fire and keep warm. Grill baguette slices over charcoal fire and season with salt and fresh pepper.

TO SERVE, place baguette slices on a plate and top with shrimp removed from the skewer. Pour tomato mixture over that and serve with lemon.

Serves 4

Mustard-Dusted Ruby Red Trout

with Colorado Corn & Beet Salad

Ingredients

- *4 6- ounce ruby red trout filets, skinless*
- *salt and pepper to taste*
- *2 ounces ground mustard seeds*
- *1 tablespoon olive oil*
- *Colorado Corn & Beet Salad (recipe follows)*
- *Opal Basil Emulsion (recipe follows)*

Preparation

SEASON trout with salt and pepper, and lightly dust the presentation side of the trout with ground mustard seeds. Sauté trout on medium to high heat in olive oil until golden brown. Turn trout over to finish cooking.

TO SERVE, place a portion of the Colorado Corn & Beet Salad on a plate. Place the trout next to the salad and drizzle the Opal Basil Emulsion over both.

Serves 4

For the Colorado Corn & Beet Salad

- *6 ears Colorado sweet corn*
- *salt and pepper to taste*
- *¼ cup olive oil*
- *8 candy-striped beets*
- *5 leaves opal basil*
- *1 ounce fig balsamic vinegar*

HEAT oven to 350 degrees. Separate corn kernels from the cob and lightly coat with olive oil. Season mixture with salt and pepper and roast on a sheet pan until slightly browned. Remove the tops from the beets and boil in slightly salted water until knife tender. Shock the beets in ice water until cooled. Remove skin and slice into ⅛-inch rings. Chiffonade 5 leaves of opal basil and mix with roasted corn and beets. Add fig balsamic vinegar and combine thoroughly.

For the Opal Basil Emulsion

- *1 teaspoon Dijon mustard*
- *⅓ cup champagne vinegar*
- *4 ounces opal basil, chopped*
- *1 cup extra virgin olive oil*
- *salt and pepper to taste*

PLACE the Dijon mustard, champagne vinegar, and chopped basil in a blender. Turn on low and slowly add the extra virgin olive oil until emulsified. Season with salt and pepper.

Great Northern Tavern

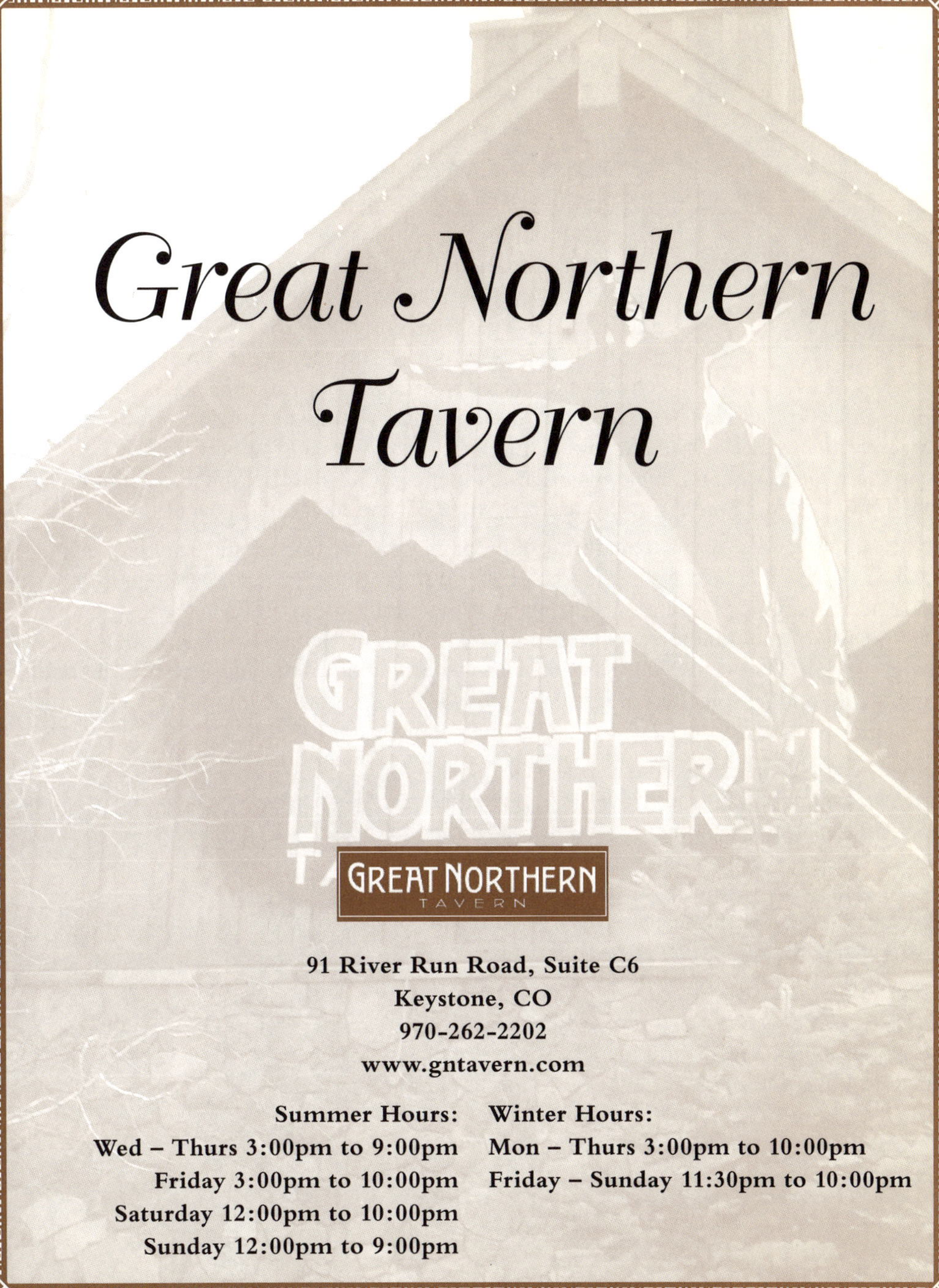

GREAT NORTHERN
TAVERN

91 River Run Road, Suite C6
Keystone, CO
970-262-2202
www.gntavern.com

Summer Hours:
Wed – Thurs 3:00pm to 9:00pm
Friday 3:00pm to 10:00pm
Saturday 12:00pm to 10:00pm
Sunday 12:00pm to 9:00pm

Winter Hours:
Mon – Thurs 3:00pm to 10:00pm
Friday – Sunday 11:30pm to 10:00pm

Great Northern Tavern

Bill Ferguson, Owner
Max MacKissock, Chef
Dan Allen, General Manager

If you already have a preconceived notion that a micro-brew pub cannot be a fine dining restaurant with white linens, great food, and a fabulous wine list, then the Great Northern Tavern is just the spot to shatter those thoughts. Located in the heart of River Run Village at Keystone Resort, the restaurant and bar offer a great meeting place before or after events on the mountain or anywhere else in the resort. The bar area features a beautiful curved mahogany bar top that perfectly sets off the display of fine spirits, considered one of Summit County's most extensive liquor collections. A large patio attached to the bar and a small patio connected to the fireplace portion of the dining room are perfect for cocktails before dinner events and other outside gatherings. As a micro-brew pub, the brewing tanks are presented behind a large glass wall.

In the main dining room, Honduran mahogany beams support the vaulted ceiling. The large brick faced fireplace in the middle of the room enriches the atmosphere with a warm glow. And the large open windows throughout the dining room and bar create a connection to the beauty of the outdoors. A proud recipient of the *Wine Spectator's Award of Excellence*, Great Northern Tavern displays part of its wine collection along the walls throughout the dining areas. A large selection of wines by the glass is also available, and the menu suggests a particular wine to accompany most of the selections on the menu.

The Great Northern takes its name from the Great Northern Railroad that ran from Denver across the upper United States. The menu reflects the traditional cuisines of these regions through interpretations of beloved trans-continental meals. A sister restaurant is located in Denver at the Denver Tech Center and follows the same theme of the Keystone location.

Chef Max MacKissock has brought his culinary expertise to the Great Northern, describing his food as regional market fresh American cuisine. Classically trained in Italy, and the fast paced restaurants of New York City, Chef MacKissock creates simple, yet elegant dishes that delight the taste buds and pair well with the large selection of libations offered.

Award of Excellence

Stuffed Calamari with Chipotle Ketchup

Ingredients

8 ounces pancetta
1 small white onion
6 ounces golden raisins
6 ounces white bread
1 cup chicken stock
¼ ounce basil
¼ ounce oregano
12 calamari tubes
6 ounces flour
4 eggs, beaten
8 ounces panko
olive oil for frying
Chipotle Ketchup (recipe follows)

Preparation

CUT the pancetta into lardoons ⅛ inch thick and ½ inch long. Sauté the pancetta for 10 minutes over medium heat. Finely dice the onion and add it to the sauté pan along with the raisins and sauté for another 8 minutes. Cut the crust off the bread and cut into cubes. Toss the pancetta, raisins, and onions with the bread, chicken stock, basil, and oregano in a large bowl.

TAKE a 1 liter plastic bottle and cut the bottom ¾ off, so that all you have left is the neck of the bottle and the rounded inch or two. Fit a calamari tube around the neck and push the stuffing through into the tube. Once all of the tubes are snugly filled with stuffing, prepare to bread them. Arrange 3 shallow bowls, one with flour, one with egg, and one with panko. Coat the stuffed tubes first with flour, then egg, and then the panko. Cover the calamari with plastic and let it sit for 2 hours in the refrigerator.

TO FINISH, heat a sauté pan with ¼ inch olive oil. Pan fry the calamari until golden brown and serve with the Chipotle Ketchup.

Serves 6

Wine suggestion: a Greg Norman sparkling white, Australia.

For the Chipotle Ketchup

2 cups ketchup
2 ounces chipotle peppers
¼ cup rice wine vinegar
½ cup honey

COMBINE ketchup, chipotle peppers, vinegar, and honey in a food processor or blender and blend until smooth.

Maine Lobster Meatballs

with Lobster Demi-glace

Ingredients

- 5 1¼ pound lobsters
- 5 eggs
- 8 slices white bread, crust discarded
- ⅛ cup flat leaf parsley, chopped
- ⅛ cup Italian basil, chopped
- ½ cup Parmesan Reggiano cheese, finely grated
- 2 cups panko
- 1 teaspoon butter
- 1 teaspoon oil
- Lobster Demi-glace (recipe follows)

Preparation

BOIL 24 ounces of water in a large stockpot and cook the lobsters one at a time for 2 ½ minutes each. Pull all the meat and innards out of the lobsters. Reserve the meat and bodies and throw away the innards.

IF YOU have a meat grinder, grind the meat on a medium setting. If you do not have a meat grinder just finely chop the lobster. Place it in a large mixing bowl. Beat the eggs and add to the lobster. Place the bread in a food processor and blend until you have small crumbs. Add the crumbs, parsley, basil, and Parmesan to the lobster and fold gently. Roll the lobster between your two palms into the size of golf balls. Then roll the balls in panko and place on parchment paper.

IN A medium sauté pan, add the butter and oil, and cook the meatballs, 6 at a time, over medium high heat until they are crispy on all sides. Toss the meatballs with a little Lobster Demi-glace and serve 3 per portion for a wonderful appetizer, or 6 per person for an entrée. They are also very tasty served over pasta.

Serves 6 as an appetizer

Wine suggestion: Condes de Albarei, Albarino, Spain

For the Lobster Demi-glace

- 3 carrots,diced
- 1 head celery,diced
- 2 fennel bulbs, diced
- 2 large yellow onions, diced
- 2 beefsteak tomatoes, diced
- 2 stalks lemongrass, minced
- 1 tablespoon oil
- 5 lobster bodies, see above
- 1 cup dry white wine
- 1 tsp whole black pepper
- 2 cups heavy cream
- 1 ounce fresh tarragon

PLACE the oil in a large stockpot, and add the vegetables and lemongrass. Sauté for 10 minutes, then add the lobster bodies and continue to sauté for another 10 minutes. Add the white wine and black pepper and add enough water to cover. Reduce the heat to medium, cover, and cook for 1 hour and 15 minutes. Remove your stock from the heat and pour it through a sieve. Use a meat tenderizer to smash the lobster bodies as you push against the sieve, in order to extract all of the lobster flavor. Place the strained stock back on the stove and let it reduce by half on low heat. Then add the cream and tarragon and let it reduce by ¼. Taste and add salt if necessary. Keep warm for service.

Mint Tea Marinated Lamb Loin

with Edamame Purée

This recipe is a variation of the classic combination of mint and lamb. If you use a good quality tea and Colorado lamb, you will taste the difference.

Ingredients

- *6 Colorado lamb loins*
- *8 mint tea bags, preferably Tazo*
- *4½ cups water*
- *3 tablespoons honey*
- *2 ounces fresh ginger root, minced*
- *3 stalks lemongrass, minced*
- *salt and pepper to taste*
- *2 tablespoons olive oil*
- *Edamame Purée (recipe follows)*

Preparation

BEGIN by heating the water for the marinade to a boil. Add the tea and remove from the heat. Let the tea steep for 5 minutes, remove the tea bags, and add honey, ginger root, and lemongrass. Let it chill in the refrigerator for 30 minutes.

PLACE the lamb in a large resealable plastic bag, and pour in enough tea to cover the lamb. Seal the bag and return it to your refrigerator for 5-7 hours.

REMOVE the lamb from the marinade and season with salt and pepper. Heat a medium sauté pan over high heat and add the olive oil. Sear the lamb for 2 minutes on either side for medium rare. To serve, thinly slice the lamb and lay each portion over 2 ounces of the Edamame Purée.

Serves 6

Wine suggestion: Rosemount, Mountain Blue, Shiraz-Cabernet, Australia

For the Edamame Purée

- *16 ounces edamame beans*
- *13 ounces vegetable stock or bouillon*
- *5 ounces heavy cream*
- *1 tablespoon salt*

COMBINE the edamame, vegetable stock, and salt in a medium saucepan. Over medium high heat simmer the beans until tender, about 35 – 40 minutes. Pour the beans and stock into a blender or food processor and purée until smooth. Pour the mixture through a fine mesh sieve or chinois. Return to low heat.

IN A different saucepan, gently heat the cream until it is simmering. Slowly whisk the cream into the bean purée, and salt to taste.

Dark Chocolate Pot Du Crème

Ingredients

4 egg yolks
⅓ cup granulated sugar
1 pint heavy cream
1 teaspoon vanilla extract or 1 vanilla bean, halved
8 ounces dark semi-sweet chocolate, chopped
shaved chocolate & fresh whipped cream, for garnish

Preparation

HEAT oven to 340 degrees. In a stainless steel bowl whisk the egg yolks until the whisk leaves a trail in the eggs, and the yolks have doubled in volume. Add the sugar and mix until the sugar is incorporated. Heat the cream with the vanilla over medium heat until the cream has reached a simmer. Add the chopped chocolate to the cream mixture, and stir until all the chocolate has melted.

TEMPER the yolks by slowly drizzling ½ the cream mixture in a slow and steady stream to the eggs while whisking. When finished, combine the egg and cream mixture with the remaining cream into a medium saucepan and return to low heat for 5 minutes, while stirring continuously.

WHEN the custard is finished, pour it into 6 ramekins and place the ramekins in a roasting pan at least 2 inches deep. Fill the roasting pan with water halfway up the ramekins. Cover with aluminum foil and bake for 38 minutes. Remove from the pan immediately and cool for at least 3 hours or up to 2 days, covered.

TO SERVE, garnish with fresh whipped cream and shaved chocolate.

Serves 6

Wine suggestion: Taylor Fladgate 20, Porto, Portugal

Engine 113 of the Denver, Leadville, and Gunnison Railroad at Rocky Cut near Breckenridge circa 1900.

Briar Rose Restaurant

109 East Lincoln Street
Breckenridge, CO 80424
970-453-9948
www.briarroserestaurant.com

Winter Hours: 5:00 to 10:00pm
Summer Hours: 6:00 to 10:00pm

Briar Rose Restaurant

Bill and Roe Schardt, Owners

The Briar Rose takes you to a time when Breckenridge was first built as a mining town; long before the skiers and snowboarders came to love the quaint little town in this secluded valley. Breckenridge was founded in 1859 and is the oldest continually inhabited community in the mountains of Colorado. Named after the old Briar Rose Silver Mine, which is located on top of Peak 10, the Briar continues a tradition from those long ago days. By 1900, the mine was turning out generous deposits of silver. The miners began their day as the first light of sun touched the Ten Mile Range. By nightfall, these tired and hungry men would return to town to the comfort of their boarding house that stood at 109 East Lincoln Street. In this rough wooden building they would enjoy a hearty meal, a shot or two of their favorite whiskey, maybe a hand of poker, and then on upstairs to their sleeping rooms. The word about the great meals and hospitality spread and soon visitors from neighboring towns came to enjoy the good food and warm hospitality.

As the mining era faded and the miners left the area, the boarding house was abandoned and, in later years, burned to the ground. In the early 1960s another structure was built on the land in the same style as the old mining house. She was named after the historic silver mine and dedicated to the old spirit of fine dining and drinking.

Roe and Bill Schardt have owned the Briar Rose since 1984, and continue the tradition of serving the best slow-roasted prime rib, savory steaks and game, as well as fresh seafood, pasta, and poultry. Enter the old building and step back in to another era. The tables are draped with fine linen in the Victorian era dining room, where classical paintings and fine music add to the atmosphere. An extensive wine list provides the perfect accompaniment to your entrée, or you can enjoy any of the great libations from the full bar. The lounge features the camaraderie of the old mining house, with big-game heads decorating the walls, and a 100-year-old trophy back bar with its aged diamond dust mirror. There is also a deck located off the lounge that offers great scenic dining in the fine weather of the summer months. This is a spot to enjoy mixing with the locals as well as enjoying a fine meal in the historic ambience of old Colorado.

Escargot with Maitre d' Butter

We've served escargot this way for over 10 years and our customers say it's the best they've ever had.

Ingredients

4 ounces spinach, stems removed
4 ounces Gruyere cheese
6 large escargot
1 cup Parmesan cheese
Maitre d' Butter (recipe follows)
crackers or toast points to accompany

Preparation

HEAT oven to 450 degrees. Line ceramic oven-ready escargot dish with spinach. Place sliced or grated Gruyere cheese on spinach and lay escargot over the Gruyere. Cover entire dish with a generous amount of softened Maitre d' Butter. Bake for 10 minutes at 450 degrees. Remove from oven and cover with Parmesan cheese. Serve with crackers or toast points.

MUSHROOMS may be substituted for the escargot to make this a delicious vegetarian appetizer.

Serves 2 – 3 as an appetizer.

For the Maitre d' Butter

12 ounces butter, softened
4 cloves garlic, finely chopped
2 tablespoons parsley, finely chopped
salt and pepper to taste

MIX butter, garlic, parsley, salt and pepper. Reserve for use.

Shrimp Calvados

Ingredients

- 2 ounces peeled and de-veined shrimp (13-15 or 16-20s are preferred)
- 6 ounces whole butter, softened, divided
- 1 shallot, diced
- 4 ounces fresh rosemary
- 4 ounces Calvados brandy
- 2 cups apple juice concentrate
- ½ pound feta cheese crumbles

Preparation

PRE-HEAT pan on high, add 2 ounces butter and shrimp and quickly sear on one side. Add shallot, rosemary, and deglaze pan with Calvados. Turn shrimp and add apple juice concentrate, reducing until caramelized. Whisk in remaining butter and top with feta cheese. Garnish with rosemary sprig. Take care not to overcook the shrimp.

Serves 4

Wine suggestion: we like this dish with a Sauvignon Blanc.

Stuffed Colorado Striped Bass
with Peaches & Blackberries

Ingredients

- 4 *ounces clarified butter, divided*
- 1 *pound cream cheese, softened*
- 1 *fresh peach, finely chopped*
- 1 *small flat of fresh blackberries, finely chopped*
- 2 *tablespoons vanilla*
- ½ *cup sugar*
- 4 *8-ounce Colorado striped bass filets (with belly fat trimmed)*
- *melted butter*
- *peaches and blackberries for garnish*

Preparation

HEAT oven to 450 degrees. Mix 2 ounces of the clarified butter, cream cheese, peach, blackberries, vanilla, and sugar into a smooth consistency and set aside. Slice fish filets on the bias lengthwise, taking care not to cut through the fish. Stuff with cream cheese mixture and coat with the remaining clarified butter. Spray a pan with non-stick spray and bake at 450 degrees for 6 minutes.

TO SERVE, garnish with fresh peaches and blackberries.

Serves 4

Wine suggestion: a Sauvignon Blanc compliments this dish well.

Blanquette of Veal

Ingredients

- 1½ *pounds veal tenderloin*
- 12 *ounces whole butter, divided*
- 2 *large portobello mushrooms*
- 1 *cup pearl onions*
- 6 *ounces leeks*
- 2 *cloves garlic, finely chopped*
- 2 *tablespoons fresh parsley, finely chopped*
- 10 *ounces Madeira wine*
- 6 *ounces veal demi-glace*

Preparation

POUND the veal tenderloin into ½ inch thick medallions. Cut the mushrooms into ½ inch cubes, and slice the leeks lengthwise into thin strips. Pan sear veal medallions in 6 ounces of butter on one side until browned. Turn medallions and add mushrooms, onions, leeks, garlic, and parsley, and cook until meat is browned. Remove veal from pan and keep warm. Deglaze the pan with Madeira wine and reduce by half. Add the veal demi-glace, bring to a simmer, and pull off the heat. Whisk in remaining 6 ounces of softened butter.

TO SERVE, place the vegetables and sauce on individual plates and top with the veal tenderloin.

Serves 4

Wine suggestion: a chilled Chardonnay compliments this entrée well.

Wild Mushroom Brandied Elk Tenderloins

Ingredients

- 2 *shallots, finely chopped*
- 4 *ounces butter, divided*
- *salt & pepper to taste*
- ½ *pound assorted wild mushrooms, rough chop*
- 1½ *cups Burgundy wine*
- 4 *cups demi-glace*
- 1½ *pounds elk tenderloin*
- 4 *ounces brandy*

Preparation

LIGHTLY sauté the shallots in 2 ounces of the butter until lightly browned. Season with salt and pepper and add mushrooms and burgundy. Reduce by half. Add demi-glace and simmer until thickened. Set aside.

TRIM tenderloins into 2-ounce medallions, quickly sear on both sides in the remaining butter, and deglaze pan with brandy. Add mushroom burgundy demi-glace and simmer on low heat until desired temperature is reached. Example: simmer 2 minutes for rare, 8 minutes for medium well. Elk is best when prepared medium or less.

Serves 4

Wine suggestion: enjoy a Merlot with this entrée.

View of the porch of the Denver Hotel in Breckenridge circa 1900 with a huge snowbank of fresh snow crowding in.

Hearthstone
Restaurant
HEARTHSTONE
restaurant
130 S. Ridge Street
Breckenridge, CO 80424
970-453-1148
www.stormrestaurants.com
Open Nightly
Happy Hour starting at 4:00pm
Dinner starting at 5:30pm

Hearthstone Restaurant

Alexandra Storm & Dick Carleton, Owners
Bruce Carlton, Executive Chef
Andy Champion, Chef de Cuisine

Located on the hillside facing the ski slopes, Hearthstone Restaurant has been a favorite of locals since its opening in 1989. The owners, Alexandra Storm and Dick Carleton, have been part of the Breckenridge community for a long time, starting with their first restaurant, Mi Casa, in 1981. They also own Hearthstone Catering and handle many of the town's large events.

The beautiful old Victorian house that is the home to Hearthstone was constructed in the early 1880s as a home for Christ Kaiser, an immigrant from Germany who ran a market and butcher shop on Lincoln Street. In the late 1800s and early 1900s many prominent business owners maintained residences in this neighborhood. The building survived a fire during the 1940s and throughout the years, has been renovated to house several restaurants, including Andrea's Pleasure Palace and Whitney's Steak House.

Over the years the Hearthstone has won many accolades and awards, both for their food and for their wine list, which has received the *Award of Excellence* from the *Wine Spectator* every year since 1997. The blue and white Victorian exterior sets a romantic ambience as you climb the steps to the patio and gazebo. Inside, lace curtains frame the large windows overlooking the ski resort, and the walls feature photographs showing the history of the house. The eclectic menu features modern American cuisine, drawing flavors from all over the world.

Executive Chef Bruce Carlton began his restaurant career at the age of 15, bussing tables in North Myrtle Beach, South Carolina. As he progressed in his culinary career, Bruce was exposed to many good chefs who were willing teach him their secrets, including South Carolina's low country cooking, Northern Italian, the tropical and coastal cuisines of southern Florida, as well as the exotic dishes of central Mexico. Chef Carlton came to the Hearthstone in 1992 and now oversees all the culinary creations at both the restaurant and the catering company.

Chef de Cuisine Andy Champion began his career washing dishes and bussing tables in his uncle's Louisiana eatery. He fell in love with the business and the easy camaraderie he found. Chef Andy started his professional career in Philadelphia, followed by positions in Portland, Oregon, the Florida Keys, and Boulder, Colorado and has been with Hearthstone since 2003.

Award of Excellence

Crab Cakes with Remoulade

Ingredients

- 1 *egg white, lightly beaten*
- ⅓ *cup mayonnaise*
- 2 *tablespoons Town House crackers, crushed*
- ⅛ *teaspoon cayenne pepper*
- ⅛ *teaspoon celery seed*
- ⅛ *teaspoon dry mustard*
- 1 *pound lump blue crab*
- *butter, to sauté*
- *Remoulade (recipe follows)*

Preparation

COMBINE egg white, mayonnaise, crackers, cayenne pepper, celery seed, and dry mustard in a bowl and mix well. Fold in crabmeat, being careful not to break up the meat too much. Divide mix into 8 equal-sized patties and sauté in butter over medium heat until golden brown and hot throughout. Serve with Remoulade.

Serves 8 cakes

For the Remoulade

- 6 *cornichons*
- 2 *tablespoons red onion, diced*
- 1 *tablespoon capers*
- 1 *tablespoon fresh parsley, minced*
- 1 *teaspoon Old Bay spice blend*
- ¼ *teaspoon white pepper*
- ½ *cup mayonnaise*

COMBINE cornichons, red onion, capers, parsley, Old Bay, and white pepper in a food processor and purée. Transfer to a mixing bowl and mix in the mayonnaise. Chill and serve with the cakes.

Spice Grilled Tuna

with Wasabi Beurre Blanc and Soy Glacé

For this recipe, you want to try to time things so that your sauce is finished about the same time as the tuna.

Ingredients

4 7-ounce tuna steaks
blackening spice to taste
Wasabi Beurre Blanc (recipe follows)
Soy Glace (recipe follows)

Preparation

COAT one side of each tuna steak with blackening spice to your taste. Grill, spice-side down first, and then turn steaks and grill to desired doneness. Tuna should be served rare to medium rare for best flavor. Serve on Wasabi Beurre Blanc with a drizzle of Soy Glacé.

Serves 4

For the Wasabi Beurre Blanc

¼ cup wasabi powder
½ cups heavy cream
salt to taste
½ pound unsalted butter, room temperature

IN A saucepan, whisk the wasabi powder into the cold cream. Note: Adding wasabi powder into hot cream will result in a bitter sauce. Slowly bring mixture to a simmer over very low heat. Simmer, stirring often until thickened. Remove from heat and allow to rest at room temperature for 5-7 minutes. Whisk in butter a third at a time; adjust salt, and serve.

IF YOUR butter is too soft, or your cream is too hot when adding the butter, your sauce will "break", that is the butterfat will separate from the milk solids and will float to the top. The only real remedy for this is starting over.

For the Soy Glacé

1 cup soy sauce
1 tablespoon cornstarch
2 tablespoons cold water

BRING the soy sauce to a boil. Mix cornstarch and water together and stir into boiling soy sauce. Boil briefly, remove from heat, and cool completely. This can be made several days in advance and held in the refrigerator.

Steak Au Poivre

with Brandy Mustard Sauce

Ingredients

- *½ cup black peppercorns*
- *4 8-ounce filet mignons*
- *¼ cup oil*
- *Brandy Mustard Sauce (recipe follows)*

Preparation

CRACK peppercorns using a mortar and pestle or a spice grinder. Pepper should be large and coarse; do not use ground pepper. Transfer to a shallow bowl. Press one or both sides of steaks into the pepper, depending on desired flavor profile. Cook steaks in oil in a large, heavy pan or griddle over medium high heat until desired internal temperature is reached. This is best done outdoors if possible as the pepper tends to smoke quite a bit.

Serves 4

For the Brandy Mustard Sauce

- *½ cup brandy*
- *2½ cups heavy cream*
- *2 tablespoons country style Dijon mustard*
- *1 teaspoon salt*

HEAT the brandy in a heavy 2-quart saucepan over low heat. Simmer until reduced in volume by half. Brandy is flammable, do not leave unattended. Add cream, mustard, and salt to taste, whisk together, and bring to a boil. Continue cooking at low boil, whisking occasionally, until reduced by ½ to ⅔ depending on desired thickness. Plate steaks and serve with sauce over the top.

Garlic Granola Crusted Elk Chop

with Blackberry Demi-Glace

Demi-Glace, a concentrated reduced veal stock, can be purchased at specialty food markets.

Ingredients

- ½ *cup garlic flavored olive oil*
- 2 *cups plain oat granola*
- *salt to taste*
- *black pepper to taste*
- 1½ *cups Japanese breadcrumbs*
- 8 *8-10 ounce elk rib chops with bone, frenched*
- ½ *cup vegetable oil*
- *Blackberry Demi-Glace (recipe follows)*

Preparation

HEAT garlic oil in a heavy 2-quart saucepan. Remove oil from heat, stir in granola, salt, and pepper. Stir until oil has coated the granola well. Line a cookie sheet with paper towels, and transfer the mixture to the sheet to drain and cool. When cooled to room temperature, purée in food processor with breadcrumbs. Transfer to a broad, shallow bowl.

PRESS both sides of the elk chops into granola crust. Heat vegetable oil over medium high heat until very hot. Sauté chops in oil 1-2 minutes on each side to set the crust. Reduce heat to medium and continue cooking and turning chops to desired doneness. Plate with the Blackberry Demi-Glace.

Serves 4

For the Blackberry Demi-Glace

- 1 *tablespoon butter*
- 1 *pint fresh blackberries*
- 1½ *cups demi-glace*
- *salt to taste*

IN A heavy saucepan, heat the butter on medium heat until melted and just beginning to separate. Add blackberries and sauté until they start to release some juice. Add demi-glace and salt to taste. Reserve on low heat until ready to plate the elk.

Raspberry White Chocolate Bread Pudding

with Myer's Rum Caramel Sauce

At the restaurant, we make our caramel sauce from scratch. While this sauce is fairly straightforward, it can be a bit tricky if you have not worked with sugar before. Therefore, I have included this much-easier simplified home version.

Ingredients

- ¾ *cup egg yolks*
- 2 *cups heavy cream*
- 1½ *cups half and half*
- ½ *cup sugar*
- 1 *pound thick cut bread, such as Texas toast*
- 4 *ounces white chocolate, chopped*
- ½ *pints raspberries*
- *non-sticking cooking spray*
- *Myer's Rum Caramel Sauce (recipe follows)*

Preparation

HEAT oven to 300 degrees. In a large bowl mix egg yolks, cream, half and half, and sugar until the sugar is dissolved. Dice thick bread into 1-inch pieces. Mix bread and white chocolate with cream and egg mixture. Gently fold in raspberries last, so that their color does not bleed into entire mix. Transfer mix into 9x11-inch baking dish sprayed with the non-stick cooking spray. Bake at 300 degrees for 30 to 40 minutes, rotating halfway through cooking. Remove from oven and let cool 15 minutes before serving. This dish can be cooled completely, refrigerated, and reheated if desired.

Serves 6

For the Myer's Rum Caramel Sauce

- 2 *cups high quality caramel topping for ice cream*
- ¼ *cup Myer's Dark Rum*

MIX caramel and rum in a small saucepan over low heat. Serve warm, not boiling, over or under bread pudding.

View of the historic Hearthstone house.

Dining at the Hearthstone Restaurant.

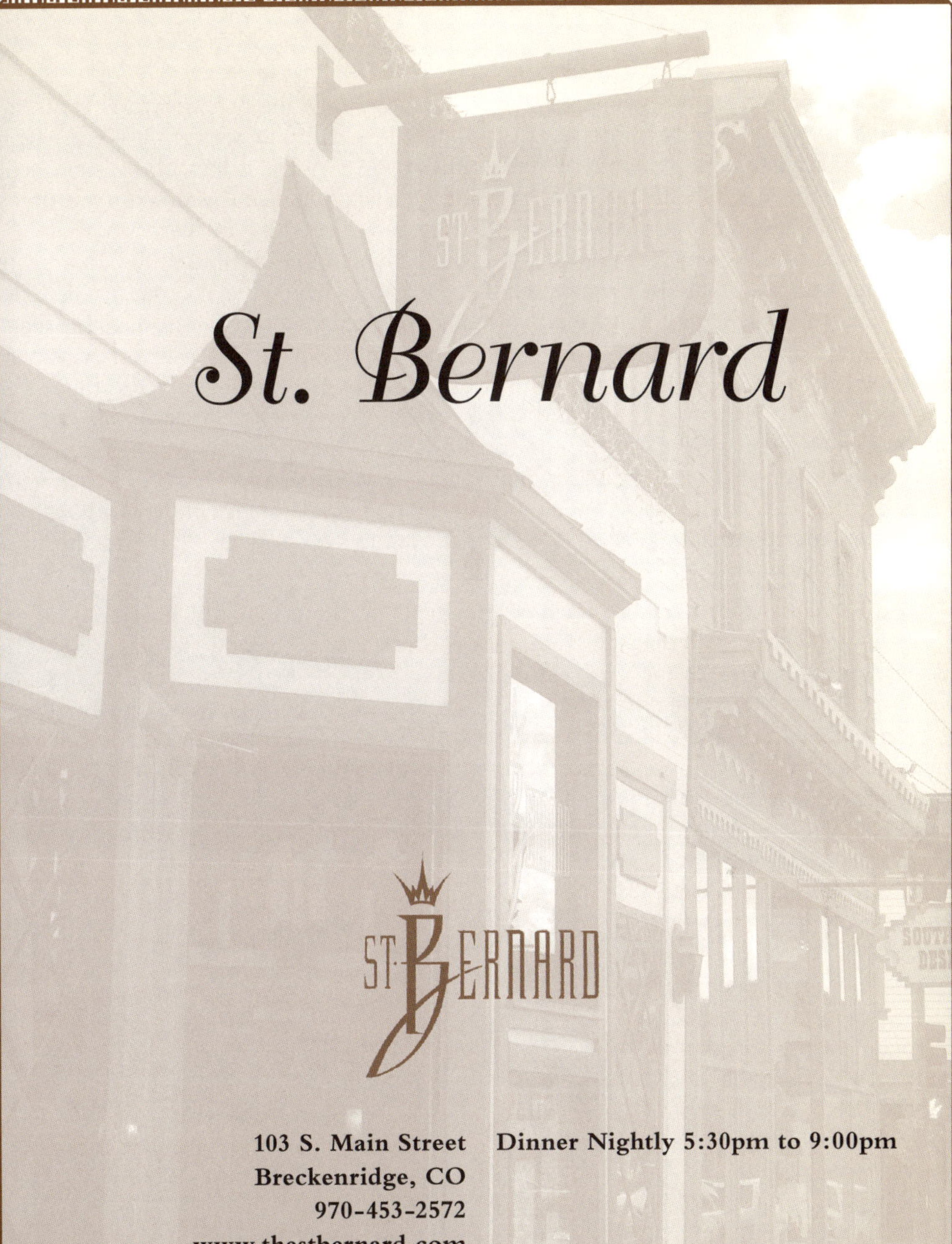

St. Bernard

103 S. Main Street
Breckenridge, CO
970-453-2572
www.thestbernard.com

Dinner Nightly 5:30pm to 9:00pm

St. Bernard

Tom Bauder, Owner

For a delicious taste of the fine cuisine of northern Italy, the St. Bernard Restaurant in Breckenridge is a perfect choice. The building in which the restaurant is housed has a long and interesting past. Originally built in 1880, it was a mercantile store selling necessities for the miners who had come to work the silver mines in the area. By the summer of 1899, the building had been converted into a grocery store, one of the many that would inhabit the space in the years to come. In 1900, the Summit County Journal announced that the building had been "rebuilt", with the entire façade undergoing a change that is similar to its current front. In 1908 it housed a pharmacy and remained as such throughout the 20s and 30s and featured a marble ice cream soda fountain, which was a favorite attraction with the locals. In the 1950s, Al Horn ran Horn's Bar in the building. At the time it was considered "a wild place for miners and singles" and survived into the early 60s when the Breckenridge economy revivified with the sport of skiing. With the new emphasis on skiing, Atila Gyarmathy opened a Gasthaus serving Hungarian Goulash and fried bread to the après ski crowd of the 60s. After a brief stint as a southern fried chicken place in the late 60s, the St. Bernard took over the building in 1971 and has proven to be a popular dining establishment for the past 35 years.

The St. Bernard prides itself in providing provincial northern Italian dining in an intimate yet casual atmosphere. The cuisine features veal, beef, game, seafood, flat egg pastas, rice, and the delicate sauces of the region. Emphasis is on fresh ingredients and dishes made from scratch. The beef and lamb are cut to order, breads are baked fresh daily, and the egg pastas are made fresh and rolled and cut by hand. Stocks and broths are made from fresh ingredients and thickened by reduction with no use of commercial stock bases. The provincial recipes are adapted from the traditions of the great Italian cities and regions, featuring the egg pastas of Bologna, the beef dishes of Piedmont and Tuscany, the seafood of Venice, the veal dishes of Florence, Milan, and Parma, the lamb of Emilia-Romagna, and the game dishes of Milan. The wine list has won numerous *Wine Spectator* awards and is replete with wonderful selections, including a very extensive list of Italian wines that pair very well with the culinary offerings.

Brie Salad
with Raspberry Vinaigrette

Ingredients

- *1 pound fresh spinach*
- *¼ cup mandarin oranges*
- *¼ cup sliced red apple*
- *⅛ cup sliced red onion*
- *⅛ cup mixed nuts*
- *¼ pound Brie*
- *Raspberry Vinaigrette (recipe follows)*

Preparation

HEAT oven to 300 degrees. Combine spinach, oranges, apples, onions, and nuts with ¼ cup of the Raspberry Vinaigrette and place on a large plate. Melt the Brie in the oven and place on top of the salad.

Serves 4

For the Raspberry Vinaigrette

- *¼ cup red wine vinegar*
- *½ cup fresh raspberries*
- *2 tablespoon honey*
- *1 tablespoon fresh thyme*
- *1 tablespoon fresh tarragon*
- *1 cup blended olive oil*
- *salt and white pepper to taste*

COMBINE vinegar, raspberries, honey, thyme, and tarragon in a blender. Blend on high and slowly add the oil until combined. Add salt and white pepper to taste.

Seafood Cannelloni

with Lobster Cream Sauce

Ingredients

- *¼ pound 16-20 shrimp*
- *¼ pound lobster meat*
- *¼ pound salmon*
- *¼ pound halibut*
- *vegetable oil for sautéing*
- *1 lemon, juice from*
- *2 cups ricotta cheese*
- *¼ cup Parmesan cheese, grated*
- *1 egg*
- *1 tablespoon fresh basil, chopped*
- *1 teaspoon garlic, chopped*
- *8 fresh sheets of pasta (6 inches x 6 inches)*
- *Lobster Cream Sauce (recipe follows)*

Preparation

HEAT oven to 350 degrees. Chop shrimp, lobster, salmon, and halibut, and sauté in a small amount of oil with the lemon juice. Blend the ricotta, Parmesan, egg, basil, and garlic. Mix the seafood and cheese mixture together and salt and pepper to taste. Roll the mixture into the fresh pasta and bake for 7 minutes until golden brown. Serve with the Lobster Cream Sauce.

Serves 4

For the Lobster Cream Sauce

- *2 cloves garlic, chopped*
- *1 shallot, diced*
- *2 cups lobster stock*
- *½ gallon heavy cream*
- *salt and pepper to taste*

SAUTÉ the garlic and shallot. Add stock and reduce by half. Add the heavy cream and reduce until it thickens. Season with salt and pepper.

Pappardelle Tartufo Bianco

Ingredients

- ¼ *cup olive oil*
- ¼ *pound portobello mushrooms, sliced*
- ¼ *pound shiitake mushrooms, sliced*
- ¼ *pound oyster mushrooms*
- ¼ *cup roasted garlic*
- 1 *pound stemless baby spinach*
- 1 *pound pappardelle pasta, cooked*
- ¼ *cup white truffle oil*
- 3 *tablespoons grated Parmesan cheese*
- *salt and pepper to taste*

Preparation

IN A large sauté pan with the olive oil, cook the mushrooms at high heat until golden brown. Add the roasted garlic and baby spinach and cook until wilted. Add cooked pappardelle pasta and finish with truffle oil and Parmesan cheese. Season with salt and pepper to taste.

Serves 4 – 6

Chicken Marsala

Ingredients

- 1 pound chicken breast
- flour for dredging
- ¼ cup olive oil
- 3 small white mushrooms, sliced
- 1 portabella mushroom, sliced
- 3 shiitake mushrooms, sliced
- 1 tablespoon garlic, chopped
- ½ cup Marsala wine
- ½ cup demi-glace or stock
- salt and pepper to taste

Preparation

POUND the chicken breast until thin, and then dredge it in flour. In a large sauté pan with olive oil cook the chicken until golden brown. Add mushrooms and brown lightly. Add garlic and deglaze with Marsala. Add demi-glace or stock and reduce by 1/3. Salt and pepper to taste.

Serves 2

Alexander's on the Creek

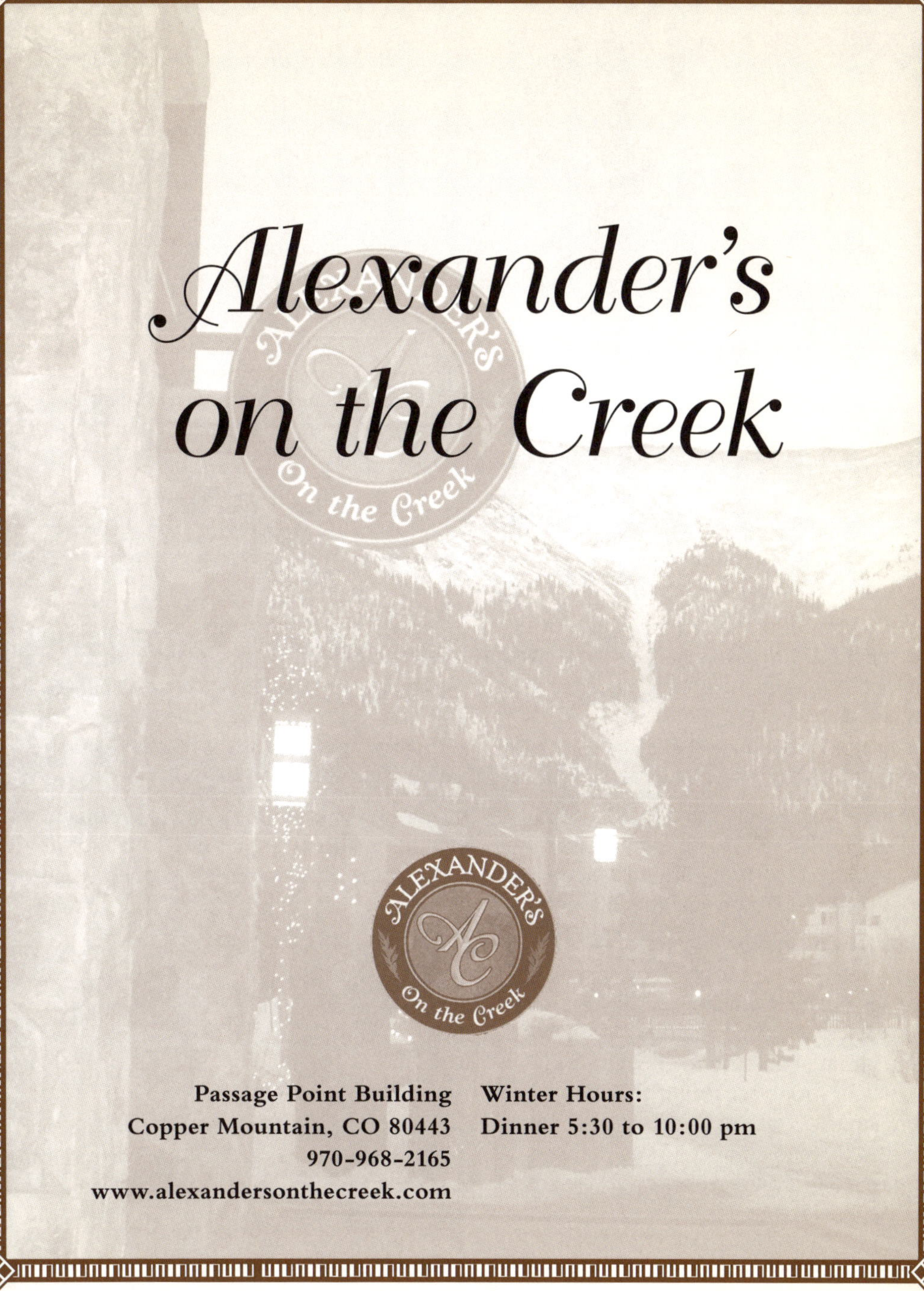

Passage Point Building
Copper Mountain, CO 80443
970-968-2165
www.alexandersonthecreek.com

Winter Hours:
Dinner 5:30 to 10:00 pm

Alexander's on the Creek

Robert Coleman, Proprietor

A veteran of over forty years in the restaurant business, Robert Coleman has created a special ambience at Alexander's on the Creek. Robert worked for Vail Resorts for many years, as well as consulting for major ski resorts across the continental United States and Alaska. At Copper Mountain Resort, and with his partnership with Intrawest Resorts, he finally found the perfect place for his dream restaurant. Robert wanted a place that would be elegant but whimsically relaxed; the perfect place after an invigorating day in the mountains of Colorado. He envisioned an upscale restaurant serving American food with an international flair.

The soft earth tones of the interior, along with the muted lighting, set off the linen draped tables set with fine wine glasses. The large floor-to-ceiling windows look out on Ten Mile Creek that flows by the building, and the crackling fire in the slate-fronted fireplace adds to the warmth and coziness.

The menu offers a nice selection of eight to ten entrées, including such favorites as Elk Filet Mignon, Chilean Sea Bass, Veal Osso Bucco, and Seared Duck Breast with Leg Confit. The appetizers include such elegant fair as Hudson Valley Foie Gras with a Vanilla Bean & Holland Rhubarb Compote and Riesling Syrup. Be sure to save room for the desserts that are all made in house daily, including the Chocolate Soufflé with Chambord Ganache and Raspberry Crème Anglaise and the luscious Caramelized Apple Napoleon.

Wines are a special treat. Part of Robert's philosophy is to serve quality wines at reasonable prices. The Verre de Vinne system at Alexander's allows great wine to be sold by the glass without worrying about the longevity of the open bottle; extracting the oxygen back out of the bottle to preserve its integrity.

Robert Coleman's Texas roots are at the base of his restaurant philosophy; one that involves creating a feeling of being a guest in a very comfortable and hospitable home. He has trained his staff to encourage guests to ask questions regarding the wines and the culinary offerings, and to make them feel that there is no need to rush. Based on the fact that many quests drive from Vail and Aspen to enjoy the Copper Mountain restaurant, it seems that he has fulfilled his dream.

Prince Edward Island Mussels

Ingredients

- 1-1½ *pounds fresh mussels*
- 1 *tablespoon oil*
- 1 *tablespoon garlic, finely chopped*
- 2 *tablespoons shallots, thinly sliced*
- 1 *teaspoon kosher salt*
- ½ *teaspoon fresh black pepper*
- ¼ *teaspoon fresh rosemary, finely chopped*
- ¼ *teaspoon fresh thyme, finely chopped*
- ¼ *teaspoon crushed red pepper*
- 1 *cup white wine, one that you would drink*
- ¼ *cup sweet vermouth*
- 1 *tablespoon butter*
- 1 *tablespoon whole grain mustard or Dijon mustard*

Preparation

IN A sauté pan on medium high heat, heat oil until it covers the bottom. Add garlic, shallots, salt, pepper, rosemary, thyme, and crushed red pepper. Sauté just until garlic and shallots start to brown. Add mussels and continue to sauté for about 1 minute. Deglaze with white wine and vermouth. Add the butter and mustard and cover. Cook for about 4 minutes. Uncover and stir to combine all flavors. Recover and continue to steam. Mussels are done when they have all opened. If some don't open, through them out.

SERVE in a large bowl with crunchy French bread.

Serves 1 for an entrée or 1-2 for appetizer

Wine suggestion: Cake Bread Chardonnay, Napa Valley, California

Pan Seared Elk Tenderloin

with Truffled Mashed Potatoes and Grilled Asparagus

This is our most requested entrée at Alexander's On The Creek.

Ingredients

- *1 12-16 ounce elk tenderloin*
- *1 tablespoon oil, preferably grape seed or olive oil*
- *kosher salt to taste*
- *fresh ground black pepper*
- *Truffled Mashed Potatoes (recipe follows)*
- *Grilled Asparagus (recipe follows)*

Preparation

HEAT oven to 350 degrees. Over medium to medium-high heat, heat oil until it is hot and covers the bottom of the pan. Lightly sprinkle the elk with kosher salt and fresh ground black pepper. Place in pan and brown on all sides. Remove from sauté pan, place in an oven safe dish, and finish in the oven at 350 degrees until desired doneness, about 8-10 minutes for medium rare. Serve on a heated plate with the Truffled Mashed Potatoes centered, the elk stacked at an angle, and the Grilled Asparagus on top.

Serves 2

Wine suggestion: your favorite Pinot Noir

For the Truffled Mashed Potatoes

- *1 pound Yukon gold potatoes, peeled*
- *¼ cup truffle oil, white or black*
- *¼ cup butter, melted*
- *1½ cups heavy cream, more for a creamier potato*
- *kosher salt and fresh ground black pepper to taste*

STEAM or boil potatoes until tender when stuck with a fork. Strain the water and place potatoes in a mixer (or back into the pot if you don't have a mixer). Add the truffle oil, butter, and heavy cream. Mix until smooth; then add salt and pepper to taste.

For the Grilled Asparagus

- *6 spears asparagus*
- *melted butter for cooking*
- *kosher salt and fresh ground pepper to taste*

PLACE on a hot grill and lightly butter the asparagus, turning to make sure you don't burn them. Then add salt and pepper to taste.

Vanilla Bean Crème Brûlée

Ingredients

- 5 *egg yolks*
- ¼ *cup plus 2 tablespoons sugar*
- *seeds from ½ vanilla bean*
- 1¾ *cup plus 2 tablespoons heavy cream*
- ¼ *cup plus 2 tablespoons milk*
- 7 *tablespoons sugar, for topping*
- *fresh fruit for garnish*

Preparation

PREHEAT oven to 325 degrees. Mix all ingredients in a medium bowl. Place the brûlée cups onto a sheet tray or cake pan depending on the height of the cups. Pour the mix into the cups. Place the tray in the oven and fill with hot water until about halfway up the side of the cups. Bake for 20 minutes and then check on them. They are done when they have the consistency of Jell-O. If they are still loose, bake longer. When they are done, refrigerate for at least 2 hours.

BEFORE serving, sprinkle about 1 tablespoon of sugar on the top of each cup and sear with a kitchen torch until golden brown. Serve on a chilled plate with fresh fruit, such as strawberries, raspberries, or blueberries.

Serves 7 Brûlées, 4 ounces each

Wine suggestion: a nice dessert wine, such as an ice wine

10th Mountain Division statue in Vail Village.

La Tour

LaTour
Restaurant & Bar

122 E. Meadow Drive
Vail, CO
970-476-4403
www.latour-vail.com

Dinner Nightly 5:30pm to 10:00pm

La Tour

Paul and Lourdes Ferzacca, Owners
Paul Ferzacca, Chef

La Tour has been in the heart of Vail for almost thirty years, and its bell tower is one of the most distinguishable and photographed structures in the town. The French Alps ambience is set off perfectly against the backdrop of the mountains surrounding Vail. In 1998 Chef Paul Ferzacca with his wife, Lourdes, fulfilled his life long dream and became the Chef/Owner of La Tour. They have decorated the restaurant with brightly color-washed walls, rich textures, and fresh flowers throughout the rooms. The walls are adorned with local and nationally recognized artwork but the vibrant atmosphere still has a rustic feel, as exemplified by the river rock fireplace.

A native of Chicago, Chef Ferzacca studied both architecture and restaurant management in college and holds a degree from the Culinary School of Kendall College. His career has been extensive, taking positions with both Spiaggia Restaurant and the Ritz-Carlton in Chicago. He arrived in Vail in 1991 as the Executive Chef of The Two Elk Restaurant atop Vail Mountain's China Bowl and transformed on-mountain resort dining in the ski industry, as he conquered the challenges of cooking at the high elevation of 11,250 feet. He has received rave reviews from the culinary press with articles in *Bon Appetit, New York Times, Rocky Mountain News, Denver Post,* and the *Wine Spectator*. In 1995, he assisted in the opening of the Game Creek Club in Vail. His love and passion for his career became evident nationally with his invitation to cook at the James Beard House in New York City.

While reaping the benefits of his star-studded career, Chef Ferzacca has given back to the industry. He donates countless hours to teaching the art of cooking to high school and college students. His students have taken first place in state competition the past two years and second place in the national contest. In addition, he has been named a "Distinguished Visiting Chef" at the prestigious Johnson and Wales University in Denver, the first Colorado chef to receive this honor.

A certified sommelier, he has trained a staff that is extremely well versed in wine knowledge, with six sommeliers on staff, more than any other Colorado restaurant. The diversified and extensive list has earned the restaurant the *Award of Excellence* from the *Wine Spectator* every year since 1998.

Award of Excellence

Escargot in Sauce Persillé

Ingredients

24 French Helix Snails (usually available canned)
4 shallots, minced
8 cloves garlic, minced
1 cup dry vermouth
2 cups heavy cream
2 bunches parsley, washed and chopped fine
6 ounces whole unsalted butter, divided
salt and white pepper to taste
baguettes slices, to accompany

Preparation

OPEN the snails, drain, and rinse well. In a large sauté pan over medium heat, sauté the snails in 2 ounces of butter with the shallots and garlic until shallots are opaque. Do not caramelize the shallots or garlic. Once shallots are opaque, add the vermouth and reduce by half. Once the wine is reduced, add the heavy cream and parsley and let it reduce to a sauce consistency or nappe. When the sauce coats the back of a spoon, remove from heat and mount the remaining butter into the sauce. Finish with salt and white pepper to taste. Serve with a baguette to sop up the sauce!

Serves 4

Wine suggestion: French Champagne

Torchon of Foie Gras

with Persimmon Marmalade, Micro Amaranth Salad, Pomegranate Vinaigrette, and Toasted Brioche

Ingredients

- 1½ pounds Grade A foie gras
- milk to completely submerge foie gras
- 2 teaspoons kosher salt
- 1 teaspoon sugar
- ½ teaspoon white pepper, ground
- ¼ teaspoon pink salt
- 2 quarts chicken stock
- Persimmon Marmalade (recipe follows)
- Toasted Brioche (recipe follows)
- Micro Amaranth Salad with Pomegranate Vinaigrette (recipe follows)

Preparation

MARINATE the foie gras in milk for 24 hours to draw out the blood. After 24 hours, remove from the milk, rinse, and pat dry. Let stand at room temperature for about 1 hour or until soft and pliable. Clean foie gras of veins. Pull apart the two lobes. Without breaking foie gras in half, gently split foie down the middle to reveal the vein structure. With a small knife or your fingers gently remove all the veins.

MIX the kosher salt, sugar, white pepper, and pink salt together. Use the dry rub to season each piece of foie gras. Marinate the foie gras in a tight fitting container for 24 hours in the refrigerator. Next day, remove foie gras from the refrigerator and let it come to room temperature, approximately 1 hour.

ONCE at room temperature you should be able to work the foie gras into a log shape, about 6 inches long and 3½ inches wide. Using a piece of plastic wrap, roll the foie gras into a log, twisting and squeezing the ends of the plastic wrap to help compact it. Unwrap the foie gras, discard the plastic wrap, and transfer the log to a piece of cheesecloth. Cheesecloth should be 1 foot wide by 3 feet long. Roll in cheesecloth to create a tight log. Twist and tie one end with butcher's twine, then again twist and tie the other end creating a very tight log, or torchon.

BRING enough stock to cover the foie gras to a simmer in a wide pot. Place the torchon in the simmering liquid and poach for 90 seconds. Immediately remove the torchon to an ice-water bath to cool. It will have lost volume because of the loss of fat in the poaching process, so it must now be reformed. Compress the torchon, still in the cheesecloth, by twisting and tying new butcher's twine to tighten the log, returning the liver to the original density and pressing out excess fat. Wrap a new clean cotton napkin around the torchon, tie the ends of the napkin with string and hang the torchon from a shelf in the refrigerator overnight.

TO SERVE, remove the wrappings from the foie gras torchon and slice in 6 2-ounce portions. Arrange the dressed Micro Amaranth Salad on 6 plates. Sear the torchons in a skillet and place on top of the greens. Spoon a small amount of Persimmon Marmalade on top, and place the toasted brioche to the side.

For the Persimmon Marmalade

8 persimmons (about 1 quart)
½ cup orange juice
1 orange, zest from
1 cup sugar

WASH the persimmons and dry with a clean towel. Then peel, quarter, and remove core and seeds. Chop the persimmons into small pieces and place in a 2-quart saucepot with the orange juice, orange zest, and sugar. Simmer this mixture, stirring occasionally until slightly thick. Cool mixture and reserve.

For the Toasted Brioche

½ ounce dry instant yeast
12 ounces milk, warmed to about 90°F
½ teaspoon sugar
1 pound flour, divided
½ teaspoon salt
1½ ounces butter, room temperature
1 egg, beaten

HEAT oven to 350 degrees. Dissolve yeast in the milk with the sugar. Add half of the flour, mix together, and rest it in a warm place for 15 minutes. Add the salt, butter, and egg to the yeast mixture and mix well. Add remaining flour, and mix until a smooth dough is formed. Proof the dough for 20 minutes, covered with plastic wrap. Kneed dough, and roll it into a loaf pan size. Spray a loaf pan with non-stick spray. Set dough inside and proof in a warm area until it reaches ½ inch from the top of the loaf pan. Bake it at 350 degrees for about 30 minutes or until golden brown and firm to the touch. Once it is done, remove it from the pan and let it cool on the rack.

For the Micro Amaranth Salad

1 fresh pomegranate
4 ounces micro carnival amaranth
1 ounce fresh chervil
salt and pepper to taste

PEEL the pomegranate and remove the seeds. Reserve in a small bowl for garnishing. Just before plating, combine amaranth and chervil tops and season lightly with Pomegranate Vinaigrette, salt, and pepper.

For the Pomegranate Vinaigrette

1 cup pomegranate juice
1 teaspoon honey
4 ounces grape seed oil
kosher salt to taste
ground white pepper to taste

IN A small saucepot, reduce the pomegranate juice by ¾ or until it reaches a light syrupy consistency. Remove from the pot and place in a small mixing bowl. Add honey and combine well. In a slow steady stream, whisk in the grape seed oil to form an emulsification. Season with salt and ground white pepper. Reserve for plating. The vinaigrette can be made up to 3 days in advance and kept refrigerated.

Serves 6

Wine suggestion: Hungarian Tokaji Aszu 5 puttonyos

Dover Sole Meunière

with Haricots Vert, Baby Creamer Potatoes, and a Lemon Brown Butter Sauce

The Dover sole is our signature dish and would be wonderful with any fish, especially some local trout.

Ingredients

- *4 ounces haricots vert, ends removed*
- *4 roma tomatoes*
- *4 whole 1-pound Dover sole*
- *salt and ground white pepper to taste*
- *1 cup all purpose flour*
- *4 ounces clarified butter or canola oil*
- *Baby Creamer Potatoes (recipe follows)*
- *Brown Butter Sauce (recipe follows)*
- *Madeira Sauce (recipe follows)*
- *3 teaspoons chives, minced for garnish*
- *2 lemons, halved & wrapped in cheesecloth*

Preparation

PREPARE the haricot vert and roma tomatoes up to 1 day in advance. Fill a 2-quart pot with water and bring to a boil. With a small paring knife, remove the stems from the tomatoes and score an "X" on the opposite end of the tomato. When water is at a rolling boil, blanch the tomatoes for about 15 seconds to just blister the skin. Refresh in an ice bath. Remove tomatoes from ice bath and let drain, keeping ice bath for haricots vert. Peel tomatoes, remove seeds, and dice. Reserve for plating.

ADD a lot of salt to the boiling water to make it taste like the ocean. This will retain the color of the haricots when cooking. Once the salted water is at a rolling boil, blanch the haricots for about 5 minutes or until al dente. Remove and refresh in ice bath. Once chilled, drain and reserve for plating.

BEFORE cooking the fish, have a small pot of water on the stove. Reheat the haricots vert and the potatoes in the water. (Drain when fish is just about done.) Remove the skin from both sides of the fish and fillet the meat to yield 4 fillets from each fish. This can be done one day in advance. Season the fish with salt and ground white pepper, dredge it in flour and sauté it in clarified butter or canola oil until golden brown.

TO SERVE, place the fish on a plate with the Baby Creamer Potatoes and haricots vert. Sauce the fish, potatoes, and haricots vert with Brown Butter Sauce, a small splash of Madeira Sauce. Garnish the plate with chives and diced Roma tomatoes and squeeze fresh lemon juice over everything.

For the Brown Butter Sauce

- *1 cup heavy cream*
- *8 ounces whole butter*

COMBINE the heavy cream and butter in a 1-quart saucepan, bring to a boil and reduce to a simmer. When bringing to a boil, stir occasionally and watch carefully so the cream does not boil over. Once reduced to a simmer, stir occasionally and continue cooking until the cream and butter breaks. Once this happens, you must stir constantly to toast the milk solids until golden brown. This will happen quickly, so be careful not to burn the milk solids. Once the milk solids are golden brown, remove the sauce from the pan and cool in a different container. Once cooled, but still liquid, purée in a blender to break up the milk solids. You can make the brown butter sauce one week in advance and just reheat it in a water bath when needed.

For the Madeira Sauce

- *½ bunch parsley stems*
- *1 teaspoon whole black peppercorns*
- *6 sprigs fresh thyme*
- *1 bay leaf*
- *1 ounce clarified butter*
- *1 shallot, diced*
- *1 clove garlic, minced*
- *3 ounces Madeira wine*
- *2 cups demi-glace*
- *1 ounce mushroom stems*
- *kosher salt and ground white pepper to taste*

COMBINE the parsley, peppercorns, thyme, and bay leaf into a sachet. In a small 1-quart saucepot add the clarified butter and shallots, and lightly caramelize them. Add the garlic and sweat until fragrant. Deglaze with Madeira wine and reduce by half. Add the demi-glace, mushroom stems, and sachet, and reduce to sauce consistency. Season with kosher salt and ground white pepper and strain through fine chinois. At this point the sauce can be held in a hot water bath or refrigerated for up to 1 week.

For the Baby Creamer Potatoes

- *8 baby creamer potatoes (you can substitute red bliss)*
- *1 teaspoon salt*

PLACE potatoes in a small pot and cover with cold water. Add salt and bring to a boil. Turn down to a simmer and let cook until potatoes are fork tender. Remove from water and let cool on a sheet pan. Once cool, refrigerate until needed. This procedure can be done 1 day in advance.

Serves 4

Wine suggestion: a nice Chardonnay from California

Sweetbreads in Caper Brown Butter Sauce

The sweetbread dish is what all the local chefs come to the restaurant to eat. It has the same sauces as the Dover sole, so make a little extra to try both dishes. The haricots vert, roma tomatoes, and baby creamer potatoes are also prepared as in the Dover sale recipe. Refer to that page for instructions.

Ingredients

2 pounds sweetbreads
1 carrot, sliced
1 small onion, sliced
1 stalk celery, sliced
1 gallon water
1 cup dry vermouth
1 bunch parsley stems
1 teaspoon whole black peppercorns
6 sprigs fresh thyme
2 bay leaves
2 whole cloves
12 baby carrots
4 ounces chanterelle mushrooms, cleaned & quartered if large
salt and pepper to taste
2 ounces clarified butter
2 ounces flour
4 ounces capers, drained
Baby Creamer Potatoes (see above)
Haricots Verts (see above)
4 roma tomatoes (see above)
Cipollini Onions (recipe follows)
Brown Butter Sauce (see above)
Madiera Sauce (see above)
¼ ounce chives, chopped fine
1 lemon, halved and wrapped in cheesecloth

Preparation

SWEETBREADS are the thymus glands of calves and young animals. The gland gradually disappears as the animal matures. They are considered a delicacy and are often expensive. Sweetbreads are very mild in flavor and delicate in texture. They are usually braised or breaded and sautéed in butter. Before cooking, sweetbreads should be prepared according to the following procedure.

SOAK sweetbreads in several changes of cold water for several hours or overnight. This removes blood, which would darken the meat when cooked. Rinse sweetbreads one more time from soaking overnight. Add to a 2-gallon stockpot along with the carrot, onion, and celery. Add water and vermouth. Combine the parsley, peppercorns, thyme, bay leaves, and cloves into a sachet and add to the pot. Weigh sweetbreads down with a smaller lid than would fit the pot properly, bring to a simmer and cook for approximately 10-15 minutes or until sweetbreads are firm. Remove sweetbreads and plunge in an ice bath to cool. Once cooled, place sweetbreads in a clean container on ice. This is to keep them cold during the cleaning process to remove the membrane. Sweetbreads are now ready, reserve for later. They can be kept in this stage for approximately 2-3 days in the refrigerator.

PEEL the baby carrots and place in a small pot with cold water and bring to a simmer. Cook untl tender, drain and keep warm. Over medium high heat, pre-heat a large sauté pan. Season sweetbreads with salt and ground white pepper, dredge in flour, and reserve. Add clarified butter to sauté pan, and add Baby Creamer Potatoes, Cipollini Onions, and baby carrots first. Let cook 1 minute and then add sweetbreads, chanterelles, capers, and haricots vert. Cook 2 minutes, or until sweetbreads are golden brown and heated through.

TO SERVE, plate sweetbreads and vegetables and sauce with Brown Butter Sauce and a splash of Madeira Sauce. Garnish with diced roma tomatoes, chives, and a squeeze of lemon juice.

Serves 4

Wine suggestion: a nice Pinot Noir from Oregon

For the Cipollini Onions

12 cipollini onions, peeled
1 tablespoon balsamic vinegar
2 tablespoons grape seed oil
kosher salt and ground white pepper to taste

ONE day in advance, prepare the cipollini onions. Place a 2-quart saucepot on the stove filled with water and bring it to a boil. Set up an ice water bath for refreshing cipollini onions once blanched. Season the boiling water with some kosher salt and blanch the cipollini onions for approximately 3-5 minutes or just until tender. Remove from boiling water and refresh in ice bath. Combine the balsamic vinegar, grape seed oil, kosher salt, and ground white pepper to taste, and mix thoroughly. Drain cipollini onions well and let marinate at least 1 day. They will last up to 2 weeks in marinade.

Soldiers from the Tenth Mountain Division, 87th Mountain Infantry Regiment, Company L execute an about face on skis near Camp Hale circa 1943.

Terra Bistro

TERRA
BISTRO

352 E. Meadow Drive
(Vail Valley Dr.)
Vail, CO 81657
970-476-6836
www.vailmountainlodge.com

Open Nightly for Dinner at 6:00pm

Terra Bistro

Kevin Nelson, Executive Chef
Rob Lewis, Executive Sous Chef

The Vail Mountain Lodge and Spa in Vail Village is a wonderfully relaxing hotel, with an attentive staff to make you feel at home. Located inside the lodge is the Terra Bistro, a lively, energetic room with an upscale urban décor accented with black and white photos displaying Vail history. The main dining room features a high ceiling with two stories of wall-to-wall windows that give openness to the room and allow diners to take in the beautiful mountain views. A multitude of small spotlights hang from the ceiling, creating a soft illumination to the room. There are several rooms available for private dinners, including the Mountain Room, which provides an intimate setting overlooking Gore Creek and the mountains. The restaurant is perfect for either a romantic dinner for two or a festive group of friends.

Executive Chef Kevin Nelson features a health-minded cuisine that fuses Mediterranean, Asian, and Southwestern influences with contemporary American style. The fresh seasonal menus focus on using organic produce, free-range meats, and fresh seafood. Kevin's culinary career started on Long Island, where he grew up, and where he worked at several high volume small-town and beach-resort restaurants. He trained at Long Island University and Farmingdale University. Moving to Vail in 1991, he joined Terra Bistro in 1993. Under the guidance of the bistro's chefs, he discovered a passion for a healthier approach to fine cuisine. Throughout his career Chef Nelson has continued to expand his knowledge, researching techniques and cuisines of different cultures to adapt in his menu creations. He has also attended continuing education courses at the Culinary Institute of America and has assisted Chefs preparing for events at the James Beard Foundation.

The menu at the bistro features a wide array of treats for every taste as well as an enormous selection of wines to pair with the culinary creations. With a certified sommelier on the Terra Bistro team, the restaurant features an exceptional wine list with a large selection of French, Italian, Australian, and California wines. The *Wine Spectator* has consistently awarded Terra Bistro with its *Award of Excellence*.

Award of Excellence

Warm Pistachio Crusted Haystack Mountain Goat Cheese

with Red Beets and Golden Raisins in Plum Wine Syrup

Haystack Mountain Goat Cheese is an award winning Farmstead cheese produced at a goat dairy farm just outside of Boulder, Colorado. I like serving it warmed for this dish as warming the goat cheese will mellow its flavor and give it an incredibly refined texture.

Ingredients

- *1 8-ounce log Colorado Haystack Mountain Goat Cheese*
- *¼ cup pistachio nuts, crushed*
- *Red Beets (recipe follows)*
- *Golden Raisins in Plum Wine Syrup (recipe follows)*

Preparation

HEAT the oven to 400 degrees. Cut the goat cheese log into 4 rounds. Roll the cheese rounds in the crushed pistachios until completely coated. Bake for 8-12 minutes. To serve, on a chilled plate, fan out the beet slices with a point of each slice in the very center of the plate and overlap the slices until you complete a full circle of beets on each plate. Spoon some Golden Raisins in Plum Wine Syrup over the beet slices. Carefully place the warmed cheese rounds in the center of the beets.

For the Red Beets

- *2 medium fresh red beets, tops removed*
- *1 teaspoon kosher salt*

COVER the unpeeled beets with cold water in a saucepot and add a teaspoon of kosher salt. Bring the water to a boil and simmer until the beets are tender throughout, approximately 40 minutes to 1 hour, depending on the size of the beets. Remove the pot from the heat and let the beets rest in the water until cool enough to handle. Once the beets can be held, peel them and discard the skins. Let the beets finish cooling in the refrigerator. After they are chilled, cut them in half from stem to base and then slice the halves thinly to form half circles. Reserve for serving.

For the Golden Raisins in Plum Wine Syrup

- *¼ cup golden raisins*
- *1 cup plum wine*
- *2 tablespoons apple cider vinegar*
- *1 tablespoon agave nectar*
- *kosher salt to taste*

IN A medium saucepot, combine the raisins, plum wine, cider vinegar, and agave and simmer until the liquid is reduced by ¼. Remove from the heat and let cool in the refrigerator for 2 hours. Season with salt to taste and reserve for serving.

Serves 4

Wine suggestion: Gewürztraminer

Colorado Lamb and Goat Cheese "Stroganoff"

with Grilled Onions and Toasted Hazelnuts

Traditional Stroganoff calls for ground meat and rice. At Terra Bistro we put a playful twist on the traditional by using rice shaped pasta (orzo) instead of rice. One of the ingredients in this recipe, which we use quite a bit at the restaurant, is agave nectar. This is the nectar extracted from the cactus and which can be used as a sweetener in just about anything. Agave is organic and suitable for diabetics as it has a very low glycemic index.

Ingredients

- *4 Colorado lamb chops, Frenched and trimmed lean*
- *1 teaspoon agave nectar*
- *kosher salt to taste*
- *Goat Cheese Stroganoff (recipe follows)*
- *Grilled Onions (recipe follows)*
- *1 tablespoon toasted hazelnuts, crushed*
- *2 3-inch long fresh rosemary sprigs, for garnish*

Preparation

NOTE: time your finished meal properly by starting to grill your lamb chops and onions just before you add your pasta during the preparation of the stroganoff.

COAT the lamb chops with the agave nectar and season with salt. Grill each chop to medium rare, approximately 2 minutes on each side, depending on the thickness of the chops.

TO SERVE, spoon the Goat Cheese Stroganoff into the center of your plate. Arrange the chops attractively on top of the Stroganoff, crisscrossing the bones. Place the Grilled Onions around and over the bones, sort of bundling everything together. Sprinkle with toasted hazelnuts and garnish with a sprig of rosemary.

For the Goat Cheese Stroganoff

- *1 tablespoon olive oil*
- *2 medium shallots, minced*
- *8 ounces ground Colorado lamb*
- *¼ cup peeled roma tomatoes, rough chopped*
- *½ teaspoon garlic, minced*
- *2 ounces Madeira wine*
- *½ cup chicken stock*
- *3 cups orzo pasta, cooked al dente*
- *¼ cup heavy cream*
- *2 tablespoons Colorado Haystack Mountain Goat Cheese, crumbled*
- *kosher salt to taste*

HEAT a heavy sauté pan. Add the olive oil, shallots, and ground lamb and cook until the lamb is evenly browned. Pour off the excess fat. Add the tomatoes and garlic and simmer for 2-3 minutes. Add the Madeira and chicken stock and let it simmer until reduced by half in volume. Add the cooked orzo pasta and bring it back to a simmer. Add the cream and let simmer for 2-4 minutes or until the pasta is evenly coated with cream sauce. Season to taste and finish with the goat cheese.

For the Grilled Onions

1 medium red onion, peeled and sliced into ¼-inch thick rings
olive oil to season
salt to taste

COAT the onion rings with olive oil and salt. Grill until just tender, approximately 2-3 minutes on each side.

Serves 2

Wine suggestion: Burgundy

Herb Marinated Bone-in Elk Loin

with Northern Bean and Root Vegetable Ragout in Sun Dried Cherry Bordelaise

Ingredients

1 teaspoon fresh sage
1 teaspoon fresh thyme
1 tablespoon Italian parsley
1 teaspoon shallot, minced
1 tablespoon olive oil
2 center cut elk chops, Frenched and trimmed lean
kosher salt to taste
Northern Bean and Root Vegetable Ragout (recipe follows)
Sun-Dried Cherry Bordelaise (recipe follows)

Preparation

COMBINE the sage, thyme, parsley, shallots, and olive oil. Coat the elk chops with the herb mixture and season them with salt. Grill the chops until medium rare, approximately 10-14 minutes, depending on the thickness of the chops.

TO SERVE, spoon the Northern Bean and Root Vegetable Ragout in the center of the plate. Place the elk on top of the ragout. Ladle or pour 2-3 ounces of the bordelaise directly over the elk and let the sauce run freely onto the plate.

Herb Marinated Bone-in Elk Loin, continued

For the Northern Bean and Root Vegetable Ragout

1 cup vegetable stock
12 medium Brussels sprouts, cleaned and halved
10 baby carrots, peeled and tops removed
3 shallots, peeled and halved
1½ cups Northern beans, cooked until tender
salt to season
2 teaspoons whole butter

IN A shallow pan, combine the vegetable stock, Brussels sprouts, carrots, and shallots. Cover, bring to a boil, and simmer until almost all the liquid is evaporated. Add the beans and bring back to a simmer. Season with salt and stir in the whole butter. As soon as the butter is melted completely, remove from the heat. Reserve for serving.

For the Sun-Dried Cherry Bordelaise

½ cup sun-dried cherries
2 medium shallots, rough chopped
1 teaspoon black peppercorns
2 cups Cabernet wine
2 cups veal or beef demi-glace

IN A saucepot, combine the cherries, shallots, peppercorns, and cabernet. Bring to a boil and reduce by half the volume. Add the demi-glace and simmer for 15-20 minutes. Remove from the heat and strain through cheesecloth or chinois. Return to the heat and bring to a simmer. Season to taste. The consistency of the sauce should be such that, while hot, it will coat and only slowly run off the back of a spoon. Continue to simmer and reduce the sauce until this consistency is reached.

Serves 2

Wine suggestion: serve with a bold Cabernet or Bordeaux

Beano's Cabin

BEANO'S CABIN

P.O. Box 915
Avon, CO 81620
970-949-9090

Seasonal Hours
Open winter and summer for dinner
Call for hours
Lunch served to Beaver Creek Club members only

Beano's Cabin

Steven Topple, Executive Chef

If you want the ultimate Colorado winter mountain dining experience, then Beano's Cabin is definitely the place to be. Your experience starts with a twenty-minute sleigh ride (wool blankets provided) from Rendezvous Cabin at the base of Beaver Creek, traveling through aspens and pines to a beautiful log cabin nestled in a snowy meadow at the base of Larkspur Bowl facing Grouse Mountain. The only way to enjoy all this beauty is to have windows everywhere and that's exactly how this hand-hewn cabin was built.

In summer, you have three ways of getting to the cabin for dinner. You can take a one-hour horseback ride, a horse drawn wagon ride, or a comfortable shuttle van. In the summer dinners are also served on the spacious deck, where guests can breath in the freshest of mountain air.

Beano's Cabin got its name from the original homesteader, Frank Bienkowski, who settled the land in 1919, raising lettuce and hay on his small ranch and working in the Aurora Mine at the head of the valley. The locals had trouble pronouncing his name, so Bienkowski became Beano.

The dining cabin features a stone hearth fireplace that adds a touch of coziness to the high-ceiling and wood beams of the room. The open kitchen allows the guests to observe the culinary creations as they are made. The five-course prix-fixe menu is a tribute to the best of Colorado lamb, beef, and game, as well as fresh seafood flown in from Hawaii and Alaska. The extensive wine list features over 500 wines and has been awarded the *Award of Excellence* by the *Wine Spectator*.

In 2006, Executive Chef Steven Topple brought his culinary creativity to the restaurant. A Vail Valley resident, Chef Topple came to the United States several years ago from the United Kingdom, where he received his formal education. He has served as the Chef de Cuisine or Chef de Tournament at the Wilcox Inn in South Carolina, Wolfgang Puck's Postrio Restaurant in San Francisco, the Sea Island Company in Georgia, and most recently at Wildflower at the Lodge at Vail. In January 2006, Chef Topple presented at the prestigious James Beard House in New York and he has recently published his first cookbook, "*So You Want to Impress...*" . Chef Topple loves to create fresh, exciting dishes, and also enjoys meeting and talking with his guests, making a trip to Beano's a special experience.

Award of Excellence

Asparagus Soup with Truffle Oil

Ingredients

- *2 shallots, finely sliced*
- *4 cloves garlic, chopped or crushed*
- *1 stick celery, sliced thin*
- *2 large potatoes, peeled and diced*
- *¼ cup oil*
- *3 bunches asparagus*
- *2 cups vegetable stock or bouillon*
- *2 cups spinach, washed*
- *1 ounce white truffle oil*
- *salt and pepper to taste*

Preparation

IN A large pot, sauté the shallot, garlic, celery, and potatoes in a small amount of oil. Chop the asparagus. Keep the tops for a garnish, and chop the remaining edible portions of the stalk very small so they cook evenly. Add to the pot to cook. Carry on cooking for 10 minutes.

ADD the vegetable stock over the ingredients in the pot and simmer for 35 minutes. Just before taking the soup off, add the 2 cups of spinach to the soup. This helps keep it green. Purée, using a stick blender or if using a drink blender, be careful not to fill it too much. Strain the soup using a fine strainer. Season the soup and check the consistency. Use a little more water if needed to thin soup, if desired.

IN A small saucepan, boil some water with a little salt. Add the tops of the asparagus, drain, and reserve. Pour the soup into serving bowls, garnish with the tops of asparagus and a little drizzle of good white truffle oil.

Serves 6

Creamy Seafood Chowder

Ingredients

- *4 slices of bacon*
- *2 onions, peeled and diced*
- *4 cloves garlic, peeled and crushed*
- *1 large can clam juice*
- *1 cup white wine*
- *2 quarts heavy cream*
- *2 large Yukon Gold potatoes, peeled and diced*
- *10 large scallops, diced small*
- *2 pounds fresh halibut, diced small*
- *salt and pepper*

Preparation

IN A large pot, sauté the bacon, onion, and garlic. Cook for 10 minutes until crispy and tender. Add the clam juice and white wine and reduce to almost ¼. Add the heavy cream to the pot and reduce until thick. Then add the potatoes, scallops, and halibut. Cook for 25 minutes, or until the potatoes are tender. Check the seasoning.

TO SERVE in the restaurant, we strain the chowder and reserve the potatoes and the fish filling. We make small Parmesan baskets, but these are hard to make at home, so I recommend buying phyllo baskets. Then you can reheat the filling, place it in the phyllo cups, and then pour the soup around in the bowl. Serve and enjoy.

Serves 6

Beet Marinated Salmon

Ingredients

- *1 side of salmon*
- *4 large beets, peeled*
- *2 cups salt*
- *½ cup sugar*
- *10 juniper berries, crushed with the back of a knife*
- *1 lemon, sliced*

Preparation

PIN bone the salmon fillet. In a food processor, chop the peeled beets into a small chop. Mix in the salt and sugar. Add the juniper berries. Rub the top of the salmon with the beet mix until every piece of it is covered. Lay the lemon slices on top and cure in the refrigerator for 24 hours. Wash the salmon fillet after 24 hours and slice with a large knife for serving.

Serves 12

Roast Beef Wellington

with Horseradish Potato and Red Wine Sauce

Ingredients

- 1 *beef tenderloin whole, cleaned (ask your butcher to do this)*
- ¼ *cup oil*
- *salt and pepper*
- 1 *tablespoon Dijon mustard*
- 1 *sheet puff pastry*
- 1 *whole egg, beaten*
- 1 *bunch fresh broccoli, boiled and kept warm*
- *Horseradish Potato (recipe follows)*
- *Red Wine Sauce (recipe follows)*

Preparation

PRE warm a grill or a non-stick pan with a little oil. Season the whole beef tenderloin with salt and pepper, and place it on the grill or in the pan for 5 minutes, turning occasionally. Remove the beef from the heat and let it cool down. Remember to rest all meat before you eat it, as it will taste better.

HEAT oven to 350 degrees. Brush the beef tenderloin with the Dijon mustard. Roll it in the puff pastry and brush the edge with the beaten egg. Seal and place into the oven at 350 degrees for 15 minutes, or until desired temperature for meat is reached.

TO SERVE, on a warmed plate place the Horseradish Potato in the middle, then slice the beef and place it on top of the potatoes. Place the broccoli on top. Enjoy.

Serves 4

For the Horseradish Potato

- 4 *large Yukon Gold potatoes*
- 1 *cup heavy cream*
- ¼ *cup butter*
- 2 *tablespoons prepared horseradish*
- *salt and pepper*

PEEL and dice the potatoes. In a large pot, cook the potatoes in water and a little salt until cooked. Strain the cooked potatoes and dry them by returning to the heat. Mash the potatoes, add a little of the cream and the butter until your desired consistency for mashed potatoes has been reached. Add the horseradish, and season the potatoes with salt and pepper.

For the Red Wine Sauce

- 1 *cup red wine*
- 2 *small shallots, diced small*
- 1 *tablet beef stock, dissolved to make 2 cups stock*
- 1 *tablespoon butter*

TAKE red wine and shallot, and reduce in a small pan. Once reduced, add the beef stock. Reduce again, and add the butter to bring the sauce together.

Hunters posing after a successful hunt in 1910.

Mirabelle Restaurant at Beaver Creek

55 Village Road (Hwy 6)
Avon, CO 81620
970-949-7728

Dinner Nightly 5:30pm to 10:00pm

Mirabelle Restaurant at Beaver Creek

Daniel and Nathalie Joly, Owners
Daniel Joly, Chef de Cuisine

The lovely old farmhouse at the confluence of Beaver Creek and the Eagle River is the home as well as the workplace for Daniel and Nathalie Joly. According to the local historian, Reverend Don Simonton, the farmhouse stands on the site that is believed to be the first home in the valley of Beaver Creek. That was a log residence owned by George Townsend, who settled here in the early 1880s. In 1898 the new owner, John Howard, called the location the Avondale Ranch and erected the building that now stands on the site. The residence changed hands two more times, all owners being cattlemen. The building was considered the largest residence in the heart of old Avon.

Now the charming two-story building houses the exceptional restaurant, Mirabelle. Dinner is served in three cozy rooms in which diners can relax, feeling as if they are in the Joly's home. Nathalie Joly smoothly manages the front of the house while Daniel takes charge in the kitchen. Chef Joly's culinary credentials are impeccable. A native of Belgium, he graduated from the Culinary Institute of Brussels and, at the tender age of eighteen, he was voted the best young chef in Belgium. After several years working in Belgium, Chef Joly came to the United States where he worked at Restaurant Million, Picasso, and Camberly's before joining the staff at Mirabelle in 1992 and purchasing the restaurant in 1999. That same year, Chef Joly was honored by being named a Belgium Master Chef, an elite group that has only about eighty members worldwide. He is the only Belgium Master Chef in the United States.

Chef Joly's expertise extends to the wonderful choice of wines, predominantly from France and California. The menu suggests a wine pairing for each dish, and he has trained his wait staff well about the wines. The *Wine Spectator* has consistently given the restaurant its *Award of Excellence*.

Chef Joly's culinary philosophy embraces the classic French techniques but without the heavy sauces and creams. His creative touch shows strongly in the unique presentations of his dishes. Chef Joly states, "Food is first eaten with the eyes. If the food doesn't look good, the experience can be spoiled." Most importantly, though, he is exceedingly particular about the freshness of the ingredients that go into his creations. All this combines in the finished presentations to the delight of the guests of Mirabelle Restaurant.

Award of Excellence

Dover Sole

Ingredients

- *4 Dover sole*
- *½ cup flour*
- *salt and pepper to taste*
- *2 Yukon Gold potatoes*
- *¼ cup butter, divided*
- *5 cups fresh baby spinach*
- *2 lemons, juiced*
- *¼ cup chives, chopped*
- *fresh chives for garnish*

Preparation

CLEAN the Dover sole by removing the skin from the bottom of the fish. Make a cut at the base of the tail and scrape back skin towards the head. Flip the fish over and repeat. Remove the head and the gills from the fish with kitchen scissors, and then rinse the fish in cold water. Use a clean, dry towel to remove the excess water from the fish and roll them in flour with salt and pepper. Using a non-stick pan, add a little butter and brown it. Add the fish and leave them to sear, about 3-4 minutes on each side to give a nice golden coloration to the fish.

IN ANOTHER pan heat a touch of butter. Thinly slice the potato with a Japanese mandolin and arrange the potato slices in a rosace style by overlapping each potato in a round shape until it looks like a flower. Add the potato wheel to the hot butter and cook to obtain a nice golden coloration. Using one more sauté pan, cook the spinach with a touch of water and season with pepper.

USING a circle mold set the cooked spinach in the middle of the plate. Then, with a spoon, remove the filet of Dover sole and place on top of the spinach (making sure to clean and remove all the fish bones). Using the pan used to cook the fish, add a small piece of lemon and deglaze the pan with the lemon juice and the chopped chives. Season with salt and pepper to taste, and pour on top of the fish. Garnish with the potato galette and a chive bouquet.

Serves 4

Wine suggestion: Jordan Chardonnay or French Deursault

Yellow Fin Tuna

with Orange Zest and Baby Arugula Parmesan Salad

Ingredients

- *1 pound yellow fin tuna (sashimi grade)*
- *extra virgin olive oil*
- *2 oranges, zest and juice from*
- *1 cup Parmesan shavings*
- *½ pound baby arugula*
- *4 bread dentelles*

Preparation

THINLY slice the tuna. Place it between 2 pieces of plastic wrap with a touch of extra virgin olive oil, and flatten. Place the thin slices on a plate and, using a small brush, cover with a mixture of orange zest, orange juice, and olive oil. Use the leftover orange and olive oil mix to toss with the arugula salad. To serve, place the tuna on the baby arugula and garnish with the Parmesan shavings and place a small bread dentelle on the top.

Serves 4

Beverage suggestion: Stella Artois, Belgian beer

Sautéed Halibut Filet

with Artichoke Ravioli and Watercress Coulis

Ingredients

4 tomatoes
olive oil
4 5-ounce halibut filets
2 zucchini, cut in long strings
Artichoke Ravioli (recipe follows)
Watercress Coulis (recipe follows)
truffle oil, to taste

Preparation

QUARTER and de-seed the tomatoes, and preserve them in olive oil overnight. Using a non-stick pan, cook the halibut filets for 2 minutes on each side or more, depending on the thickness of the fish, but keeping it moist in the middle. Blanch the strings of zucchini for 1 minute in boiling water, and arrange them in the middle of the plate in a flower shape. Pour the Watercress Coulis in the middle of the flower shape using the zucchini to keep the coulis from covering the entire plate. Then place the fish and the tomato petals on top and garnish with the artichoke ravioli. Drip a little truffle oil over it to finish.

Serves 4

For the Artichoke Ravioli

8 won ton skins or thin sheets pasta dough
1 egg, beaten
2 artichoke hearts

COOK the artichoke hearts and purée in a food processor. Prepare the ravioli using the wonton skins or pasta dough. Cut to shapes of equal size and place a small amount of the artichoke purée in the center. With a small brush, seal the edges with the beaten egg, being careful not to create air pockets. Cook the raviolis for 3 minutes in boiling water. Reserve for serving.

For the Watercress Coulis

1 bunch organic watercress
salt to taste
1 tablespoon butter
1 shallot, diced
1 cup vegetable broth or clam juice
1 cup heavy cream

COOK the watercress in boiling water with a touch of salt for less than a minute. Immediately place in ice water. Using a clean towel, remove the excess water. In a saucepan, melt the butter and cook the shallots for 1 minute until translucent. Add the broth, reduce by ½, and add the cream. Reduce by ⅓. Put the liquid in a mixer and add the watercress. Blend, strain, and cool in a double ice bath. Reserve for serving.

Sea Scallops

Ingredients

20 u10 sea scallops, dry pack
1 pound baby spinach
salt and pepper to taste
20 rice paper squares
2 heads broccoli flower
1 cup butter, divided
1 pinch nutmeg
2 red bell peppers, sliced
1 tomato, sliced
1 onion, sliced
1 pinch cayenne pepper
1 clove garlic, minced
½ cup heavy cream
15 leaves basil, fried
1 cup vegetable oil, optional
1 bunch Italian parsley, optional

Preparation

USING a non-stick pan, sear the sea scallops on both sides, being careful not to overcook them. Cook the baby spinach in boiling water, season with pepper and cool in an ice bath. Wrap up the scallops and spinach in rice paper like an envelope.

COOK the broccoli in boiling water, keeping the nice green color, and purée it. Add salt, pepper, ½ cup of the butter, and nutmeg to taste to make a mousseline.

BOIL the bell peppers, tomato, onion, and garlic with cayenne pepper. Purée in a robot coupe and then strain through a chinois. Add heavy cream and season with salt and pepper.

MAKE a beurre noisette (browned butter) from the remaining ½ cup of butter, and sear the sea scallop envelopes.

TO SERVE, place ring form on each plate and pour the broccoli mousseline in it to set. Remove form and rest 5 scallops on top. Garnish with the bell pepper cream mixture and fried basil leaves. As an option, you can place the parsley in a blender and blend with the vegetable oil, and then drizzle this over the top.

Serves 4

Wine suggestion: a Pinot Gris wine

Turbotin

The tomatoes may be used fresh, or they can be made into a confit, marinated in olive oil overnight.

Ingredients

- *2 bulbs fennel, with tops*
- *2 onions, chopped*
- *1 cup extra virgin olive oil*
- *1 cup clam broth*
- *4 papillote papers (parchment or other greaseproof cooking paper)*
- *4 6-ounce filets of turbotin (turbot)*
- *3 tomatoes, quartered & seeds removed, or as tomatoes confit*
- *1 bunch fresh cilantro, chopped*

Preparation

CHOP the fennel bulbs as for concasser, reserving the tops for later. Cook the fennel with the onions in olive oil. Add the clam broth and reserve.

HEAT oven to 375 degrees. Using the parchment paper, put a turbot fillet in the middle and cover with the clam broth, fennel, and onion concasser. Top with the tomatoes confit and a drip of olive oil. Repeat for the other 3 filets. Fold the edges of the papers in small sharp folds to hold the ingredients in. Bake for 4 minutes until the papers fill with steam and obtain a nice brown color.

TO SERVE, open the papillottes and serve it in bowls. Garnish with the chopped fennel tops, and the cilantro.

Serves 4

Rack of Lamb

Ingredients

- 5 eggplants
- 1 cup garlic oil
- salt to taste
- 1 sprig thyme
- 1 cup extra virgin olive oil
- 2 artichokes
- 1 lemon
- 1 cup flour
- 4 zucchini
- 6 4-bone racks of lamb
- 2 cloves garlic, chopped
- 1 thyme bouquet
- ½ cup white wine
- 1 cup demi-glace
- ½ cup unsalted butter
- 3 Yukon Gold potatoes
- ½ liter brown chicken stock

Preparation

HEAT oven to 300 degrees. Slice the cleaned eggplants through the middle. Place the eggplants on a sheet pan and top with garlic oil, salt, and thyme. Cover with aluminum foil and cook for 2 hours in the oven. When done, remove the meat from the eggplant and mix with olive oil to obtain a nice eggplant purée or caviar.

CLEAN the artichoke hearts and cook them in a blanc (a mixture of boiling water, lemon and flour) in order to retain their color. Slice into the shape of a 2 ½-inch circle. Slice the zucchini and cook with olive oil in a non-stick Teflon pan. Using a 2 ½-inch circle, put a slice of artichoke on the bottom, then the eggplant purée, then artichoke again, then a touch of eggplant mousse, and finish with a circle of overlapping zucchini slices.

CLEAN the racks of lamb and cut them in double bone sections. Brown the scraps in a saucepan. Add garlic and thyme, and deglaze with white wine. Reduce until almost dry and add the demi-glace. Strain, and finish with thyme and a touch of unsalted butter. Reserve for serving.

HEAT oven to 400 degrees. In a skillet, sear the lamb to obtain a nice crust on the skin and finish cooking in the oven for about 8 – 10 minutes.

COUNTING ½ potato per guest, cut potatoes like big Pont Neuf tourner (large 5- or 6-sided matchsticks), and then sauté with olive oil and butter. Add thyme, garlic and a little brown chicken stock (enough to cover potatoes) and finish in the oven at 350 degrees.

FOR garnish, clean and cook 1 baby carrot or haricots verts with shallot and honey. Put the lamb, sauce, potatoes, and artichoke and eggplant mousse circle together on a plate with garnish and serve warm.

Serves 6

Wine suggestion: a Chateau Neuf wine

Dessert Trio

of Tropical Trifle, Apricot Tartelette, and Chocolate Fondant

Ingredients For the Tropical Trifle

- *1 cup bananas, sliced*
- *6 cups apple juice*
- *4 cups passion fruit juice*
- *10 gelatin sheets*
- *1 cup whipping cream, whipped*
- *¼ cup genoise sponge cake*
- *Malibu rum*

PLACE the genoise sponge cake on a sheet pan and drizzle with Malibu rum to desired flavor. Combine the banana, apple juice, and passion fruit juice. Add the gelatin sheets cold, then add the whipped cream. Using a 2-inch circle form, cut 8 circles out of the soaked sponge cake. Layer the fruit juice and cream mixture over the top of the cake.

For the Apricot (or peach) Tartelette

- *7 eggs*
- *14 ounces sugar*
- *1 pound almond powder*
- *13 ounces pastry cream*
- *1 pound butter, softened*
- *8 apricots or peaches*
- *simple syrup, 1 cup water & 1 cup sugar brought to a boil*
- *1 pound sugar dough, precooked*

FOR the frangipane, mix and blanch (vigorously beat until light and fluffy) the eggs and sugar. Add the almond powder and pastry cream. Then add the butter.

HEAT oven to 350 degrees. Cook the apricots or peaches in simple syrup. Using a small form of precooked sugar dough, add the Frangipane in the base and cook with the apricot or peach mixture on top in the oven for approximately 4 – 6 minutes.

For the Chocolate Fondant

- *14 ounces chocolate*
- *14 ounces butter*
- *7 ounces flour*
- *½ cup starch*
- *14 ounces sugar*
- *10 eggs*
- *6 egg yolks*

HEAT the oven to 400 degrees. Melt the chocolate and butter over a bain-marie. Then mix the flour and starch and slowly add to the chocolate and butter. Blend the eggs and sugar and add to the mixture. Let this dough cool down. Place 2-inch circle ring forms on a baking sheet, fill with the mixture, and bake in oven for 8 minutes.

TO SERVE, place the Tropical Trifle, Apricot (or peach) Tartelette, and Chocolate Fondant on a plate together and garnish with English cream, fruit coulis, or ice cream and a Mirabelle tulip.

Serves 8

Bar and reception area at Mirabelle.

Dining room at Mirabelle.

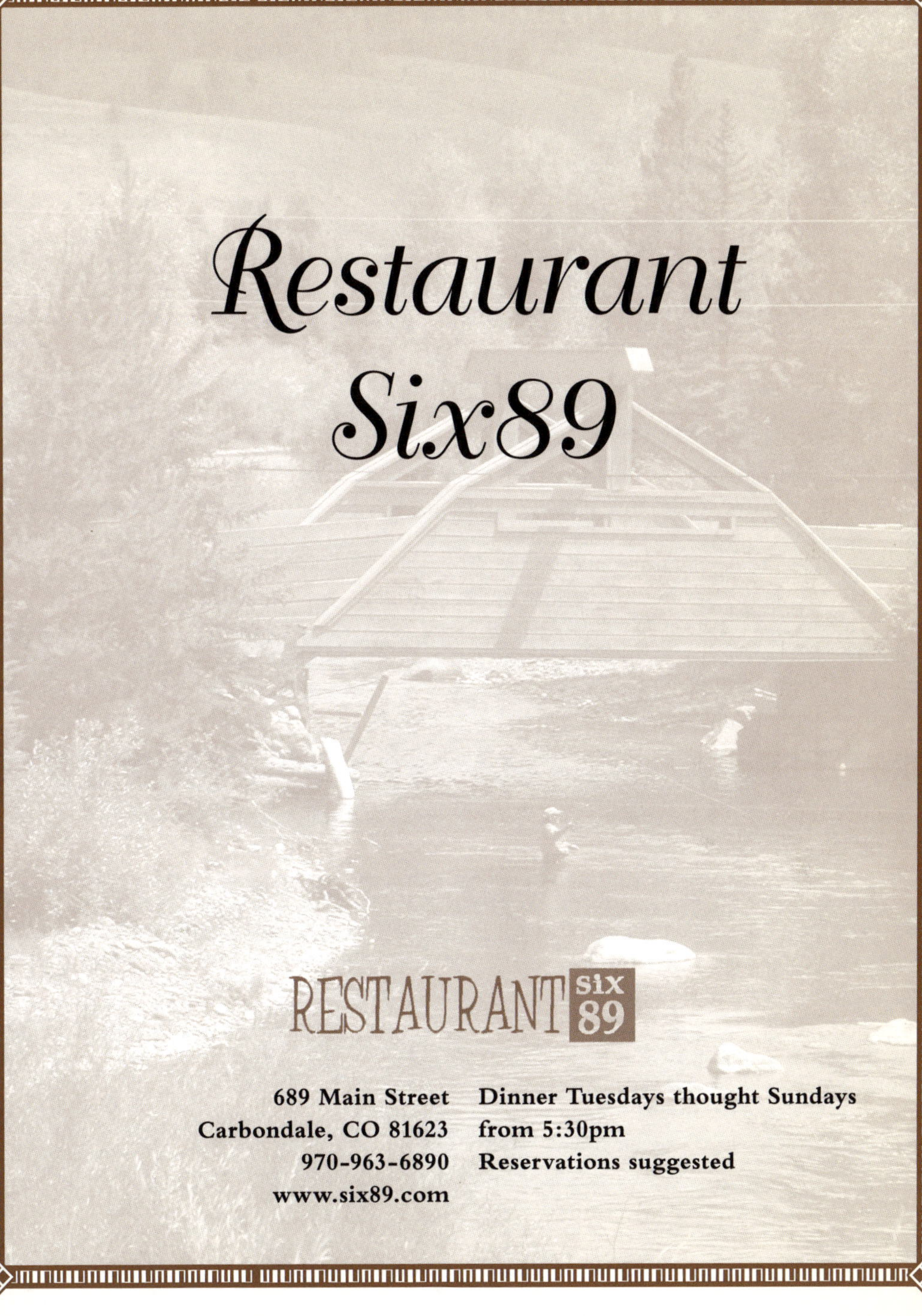
Restaurant
Six89
RESTAURANT six 89
689 Main Street
Carbondale, CO 81623
970-963-6890
www.six89.com
Dinner Tuesdays thought Sundays
from 5:30pm
Reservations suggested

Restaurant Six89

Mark Fischer, Chef/Owner

Set on the corner of Main and 7th in the small mountain town of Carbondale, you might think this is someone's beautifully cared for home if it weren't for the parade of guests strolling up the path to the front entrance, which features a glass-enclosed porch and two dining tables, perfect for a quiet, intimate meal. The mahogany woodwork, textured walls, and zinc accents as in the top of the wine bar, create a warm sense of vitality in the renovated "Old Town Carbondale" house. A redwood addition to the house offers comfortable seating with large windows. This main area contains the wine wall, enclosed in glass with redwood panels and doors. A wooden library ladder is used to access the top racks. From this room, guests step out onto the festive deck and patio area where they can dine under old blue spruce and aspen trees. Unobtrusive Italian lights hang from the inside spokes of burgundy umbrellas, adding a festive air to tables covered with white linens and candles. The fenced-in area is adorned with sculptures on the beautifully landscaped yard.

Mark Fischer opened his "kitchen and wine bar" in 1998, with the goal to provide an intelligent alternative to the fine dining experience of Aspen. After working in a restaurant following his college years, he decided to give cooking a professional try. He attended the Pennsylvania Culinary Institute and graduated as valedictorian. His culinary career includes four years at Aspen's Caribou Club, during which he served as Sous Chef and then Executive Chef. After to the Caribou Club, Mark served as Chef at San Francisco's famed Fog City Diner. He also worked in the kitchens of New York City's Mesa and Le Cirque, as well as Table 29 in Napa, California.

Chef Fischer's philosophy is to apply classically based techniques to create dishes with a global backbeat, using as many fresh ingredients as possible from the local small-scale growers and distributors. The restaurant's cooking is hardwired to the rhythm of the seasons and changes with these markets. The irreverent menu encourages the ideas of sharing and grazing through a succession of smaller plates. The award-winning wine list is organized between old world and new world wines. Chef Fischer offers his guests who order a wine by the glass a special service. The servers take the extra time to bring the bottle directly to the table to pour the requested glass, giving the guest an opportunity to view the label and learn more about their choice.

Rhubarb Martini

We offer these in the spring and early summer when wild rhubarb is growing all over.

Ingredients

4 ounces Stolichnaya vodka
1 ounce rhubarb juice
1 splash limejuice
1 sprig rhubarb
1 lime wheel

Preparation

SHAKE the liquids over ice to bruise, and strain into iced martini glasses. Garnish with a rhubarb sprig and lime wheel.

Serves 1

Goat Cheese Gnocchi over Field Greens

with Oregano Vinaigrette

This dish is even better with things like locally foraged wild mushrooms and greens and asparagus from Paonia. It's been on the menu since we opened in 1998. Attempts to replace it have met with resistance.

Ingredients

1½ pounds Yukon Gold potato "meat"
3 eggs
24 ounces cake flour
11 ounces goat cheese (1 log)
1 cup Reggiano cheese, grated
2 tablespoons kosher salt
2 tablespoons cracked black pepper
½ cup fresh oregano, chopped
olive oil to coat
8 tablespoons butter
2 cups shallots, minced
16 cups shiitake mushrooms, sliced
16 cups asparagus, sliced and blanched
Oregano Vinaigrette (recipe follows)
salad greens
white truffle oil to drizzle
grated Reggiano cheese, for garnish

Goat Cheese Gnocchi over Field Greens, continued

Preparation

HEAT the oven to 350 degrees. Bake the potatoes and cool slightly. Peel and grate the potatoes while they are still warm. Move to a mixing bowl. Add the eggs, flour, and cheeses and mix until the dough comes together. Add the salt, pepper, and oregano and mix until well incorporated. You may need to add a little more flour to make the dough easy to handle. Do not add too much flour or the dough will become too tough. Remove to a cutting board and knead by hand until the dough is of the correct consistency. Let it rest.

ROLL the dough into ropes approximately ½ inch thick and cut it into 1-inch pieces. Roll each piece with the back tines of a fork to form cute little ridges. These are traditional as well as functional. Blanch the gnocchi in salted water, drain, and chill. Toss with olive oil and remove to a container. Refrigerate until ready to serve.

TO SERVE, use a very wide skillet or work in batches, keeping the finished gnocchi warm.

HEAT the butter in the skillet until nutty. Add the shallots and the gnocchi. Cook, stirring often, until the gnocchi begins to color lightly. Add mushrooms and cook until soft. Add asparagus and heat through. Adjust the seasonings with salt and pepper and dress with Oregano Vinaigrette.

REMOVE to a serving plate and top with greens tossed with Oregano Vinaigrette. Grate some Reggiano cheese over the top and drizzle with the truffle oil. Enjoy!

Serves 16

For the Oregano Vinaigrette

1 cup shallots, chopped
½ cup Dijon mustard
1 cup fresh oregano
1 cup champagne vinegar
1 tablespoon kosher salt
1 tablespoon cracked black pepper
3 cups extra virgin olive oil

MIX the shallots, mustard, oregano, and vinegar together. Add the salt and pepper. Whisk in the olive oil to emulsify and adjust the seasonings.

Grilled Pork Chops

with Peach Bourbon BBQ and Smoked Mozz Grits

When Palisades peaches (or any other Western Slope stone fruits) are in season, this is at its best.

Ingredients

- *4 16-ounce center cut double pork chops*
- *Peach Bourbon BBQ Sauce (recipe follows)*
- *Smoked Mozz Grits (recipe follows)*

Preparation

GRILL or pan sear the pork chops to desired temperature. To serve, place a chop on each dinner plate. Scoop the Mozz Grits to the side and drizzle the Peach Bourbon BBQ Sauce over top.

Serves 4

For the Peach Bourbon BBQ Sauce

- *1 yellow onion, diced medium*
- *1 tablespoon garlic, chopped*
- *1 tablespoon oregano, dry*
- *2 tablespoons olive oil blend*
- *½ cup apple cider vinegar*
- *2 tablespoons Worcestershire sauce*
- *¼ cup molasses*
- *1 tablespoon Tabasco or other hot sauce*
- *1 quart peach purée (about 10 peaches, halved, with pits removed)*
- *½ cup bourbon (Jim Beam or Jack Daniels)*
- *1 quart chicken stock*
- *salt and fresh ground black pepper to taste*

SAUTÉ the onion, garlic, and oregano in the olive oil until soft and fragrant. Add the vinegar, Worcestershire sauce, molasses, hot sauce, and peach purée and bring to a simmer. Add the bourbon and return to a simmer. Add the chicken stock and reduce by ¼. Pass this mixture through a food mill, and adjust the seasonings. Chill and reserve.

For the Smoked Mozz Grits

- *2 cups grits*
- *2 cups chicken stock*
- *2 cups heavy cream*
- *1 cup Fontina, grated*
- *½ pound butter, cubed*
- *2 tablespoons fresh oregano*
- *salt and cracked black pepper to taste*
- *cream or milk to moisten*
- *smoked mozzarella, grated, to taste*

Grilled Pork Chops, continued

PLACE the grits in a large stainless steel bowl, cover with cold water, and stir. Skim off the chaff that rises to the top. Stir and skim again. Pour off the water and the light bran. In a large pot, bring the stock and cream to a boil. Whisk in the grits and cook, stirring often, just until the mixture begins to pull away from the sides of the pot, about 25 minutes. Remove from the heat and mix in the Fontina, butter, and oregano. Adjust seasonings. Pour the grits into a greased sheet tray and allow to cool.

TO SERVE, reduce a small amount of cream or milk in a saucepan. Add the grits and incorporate the liquid, stirring with a wooden spoon. Finish with grated smoked mozzarella, adding more or less to taste.

Rabbit and Mushroom Ragout

over Black Pepper Pappardelle

This is an awesome cold weather dish. You could replace the rabbit with duck legs if you like.

Ingredients

- *2 ounces dried porcini mushrooms*
- *750 ml red wine, preferably red zinfandel*
- *4 rabbit legs, bone-in*
- *kosher salt and fresh ground black pepper to taste*
- *flour, to coat*
- *olive oil to sauté*
- *1 cup pancetta, diced*
- *1 white onion, diced fine*
- *1 tablespoon garlic*
- *½ cup tomato paste*
- *1 bay leaf*
- *1 quart chicken stock*
- *Black Pepper Pappardelle (recipe follows)*

Preparation

COMBINE the mushrooms and red wine in a saucepan and bring to a simmer. Turn off the heat and let the mushrooms steep. Trim the rabbit legs of any excess fat and sinew. Season them generously with salt and pepper and cover with flour.

IN A large skillet, heat a small amount of olive oil. Brown the rabbit pieces in the oil, then remove to a 4-inch half hotel pan. Discard all but a film of oil from the skillet. Add the pancetta and brown over medium heat. Add the onions and garlic to the pancetta and brown. Stir in the tomato paste and cook, stirring until well incorporated. Add the chicken stock and bay leaf, stirring until the mixture and stock are evenly incorporated. Add the steeped mushrooms and red wine.

ADD this braising liquid to the pan with the rabbit, making sure all the stock has been transferred. Cover and braise for about 2 hours until the rabbit meat is falling from the bone. Remove the meat from the pan and allow to cool. Cool the braising liquid without straining. After the meat has cooled, pull from the bone and shred by hand. Add it back to the braising liquid and bring to a simmer and adjust the seasonings.

JUST before serving, bring a large pot of heavily salted water to boil. Drop in the Black Pappardelle nests and cook briefly just to al dente. Drain and toss with the ragout and serve immediately.

Serves 12

For the Black Pepper Pappardelle

8 cups all purpose flour
14 eggs
1 tablespoon kosher salt
2 tablespoons extra virgin olive oil
2 tablespoons cracked black pepper
cornmeal to dust

MIX the flour, eggs, salt, olive oil, and pepper and let rest. To roll, cut a 7-ounce piece of dough and roll through a pasta machine until the #5 setting is reached, using just enough flour to keep the process moving along smoothly. Roll through the #5 setting 2 times and allow the dough to rest briefly before cutting. Then cut the piece in half (giving you 2 pieces of 3½ ounces each). Next, cut each piece into ½-inch ribbons. Dust with an ample amount of cornmeal. Twirl into a nest and reserve for service.

Blueberry Corn Cakes
with Sweet Corn Ice Cream

Ingredients

2 cups all purpose flour
2 cups cornmeal
1 tablespoon baking powder
1 teaspoon kosher salt
1 cup granulated sugar
3 cups blueberries
4 eggs, beaten
½ cup butter, melted
2 cups milk
1 cup sour cream
1 tablespoon vanilla extract
Sweet Corn Ice Cream (recipe follows)

Preparation

HEAT oven to 375 degrees. Combine the flour, cornmeal, baking powder, salt, and sugar in a large stainless steel bowl. Add the blueberries, stirring to coat. In a separate bowl, whisk together the eggs, butter, milk, sour cream, and vanilla. Make a well in the center of the dry mix and add the liquid. Stir quickly just to moisten the dry ingredients. Don't over mix. Pour into a greased half hotel pan. Bake for 30 minutes.

TO SERVE, cut portions of the corn cake and serve with Sweet Corn Ice Cream.

Serves 16

For the Sweet Corn Ice Cream

4 cups Olathe sweet corn (about 4 ears)
1 tablespoon butter
1 pound plus 2 tablespoons granulated sugar
2 teaspoons kosher salt, divided
1 quart whole milk
1 quart heavy cream
1 teaspoon vanilla extract
1 vanilla bean, split and scraped
1 pound granulated sugar
16 egg yolks

SAUTÉ the corn with the butter, 2 tablespoons sugar, and 1 teaspoon salt until tender. Reserve. Scald the milk and heavy cream with the reserved corn, vanilla extract, and vanilla bean. Whisk together the egg yolks, remaining salt, and 1 pound sugar. Temper the cream/milk mixture into the sugar and eggs. Return to the saucepan and, stirring constantly, heat the base until it coats the back of a wooden spoon (approximately 180 degrees). Remove from the heat; pass through a food mill and chill.

TO MAKE the ice cream, add 1½ quarts of the base mixture to the well-chilled bowl of an ice cream maker. Turn just until the mixture has increased in volume to 2 quarts and is well set. Freeze for at least 8 hours before using.

Root Beer Poached Pears

with Caramel Semifreddo

Ingredients

- *12 pears: bosc, seckel, d'anjou*
- *root beer, to cover*
- *1 cup sugar*
- *1 cinnamon stick*
- *1 tablespoon vanilla extract*
- *1 pinch kosher salt*
- *1 lemon, halved*
- *Caramel Semifreddo (recipe follows)*
- *fresh mint, for garnish*
- *powdered sugar, for garnish*

Preparation

CAREFULLY peel the pears, leaving the stem intact. Square the bottoms and, using a melon baler, remove the cores and seeds. In a large saucepan, place the pears, enough root beer to cover them, the sugar, cinnamon stick, salt, and lemon. Bring to a boil, and then lower the heat to a simmer. Place a plate or lid on top of the pears to make certain they are completely submerged. Simmer until the pears are tender and remove. Cool upright. Strain the sauce and reduce to the desired consistency; keep warm for serving.

SERVE the pears warm with the reduced sauce and a slice of Caramel Semifreddo. Garnish with mint and powdered sugar.

Serves 12

For the Caramel Semifreddo

- *2 cups whipping cream*
- *1 tablespoon vanilla extract*
- *6 egg whites, room temperature*
- *1 pinch kosher salt*
- *1 cup sugar*
- *½ cup caramel sauce (or use poaching caramel from the pears)*

LINE a 10-inch springform pan with plastic wrap, with ample overhang to fold back over the top completely. Place in the freezer to chill. Beat the whipping cream and the vanilla with a whisk to medium peaks. Chill and reserve.

PLACE the egg whites and the salt into the bowl of a mixer fitted with a whisk and beat on medium speed until frothy. Slowly add the sugar in a steady stream and continue to beat on medium until the sugar has been completely incorporated. At this point, remove the bowl from the mixer and place in a water bath or over flame and gently heat the meringue, stirring constantly, until the mixture has reached a temperature of 140 degrees. Return the meringue to the mixer and beat on medium speed until the mixture has doubled in volume and cooled to room temperature.

REMOVE the meringue to a large stainless steel bowl and gently fold in the caramel sauce. Fold in the whipped cream by thirds and pour into the prepared springform. Chill in the freezer at least 3 hours. Before cutting, allow the semifreddo to temper at room temperature 15 minutes.

Maple Anglaise

Ingredients

- *6 egg yolks*
- *½ cup granulated sugar*
- *½ cup maple syrup*
- *2 cups whole milk*
- *1 tablespoon vanilla extract*
- *1 pinch kosher salt*

Preparation

WHISK together the yolks, sugar, and maple syrup. Scald the milk, vanilla extract, and salt in a medium saucepan. Temper the milk into the egg and sugar mix. Return to the heat and cook until the mixture coats the back of a spoon. Strain, cool, and reserve for serving.

Serves 12

Campo de Fiori

Campo de Fiori

205 South Mill Street
Aspen, CO 81611
970-920-7717
www.campodefiori.net

Dinner served nightly from 5:00pm
Reservations recommended

Campo de Fiori

Luigi and Elizabeth Giordani, Owners
Berto Paglia, Executive Chef/Partner
Guiseppe Garafola, Chef de Cuisine

One of the hottest places to go in Aspen for a fantastic dinner and also to see and be seen is definitely Camp de Fiori. Literally meaning "field of flowers", the restaurant's name is also the name of an informal piazza in Rome that has an open-air flower market. Step down below street level into an open-air interior court that serves as a lovely al fresco dining area during fair weather. Tables in both the interior and exterior dining areas are nestled closely together, creating a lively atmosphere, with a special camaraderie among the guests. The open kitchen and packed bar also lend to the festive atmosphere. The Giordanis hired decorative painter James Johansen to paint the restaurant's walls with whimsical trompe l'oeil paintings reminiscent of Italy. He has not only painted the walls, but the ceiling, floor, some of the furniture, and even the salt and pepper shakers. The window scenes extend the space in the restaurant, and give the diners the illusion that they are looking out at a Tuscan countryside scene.

Campo de Fiori is the brainchild of Luigi and Elizabeth Giordani along with their partner and Executive Chef, Berto Paglia. Luigi, who received his formal culinary education in Rome, develops all the menus with his Executive Chef and partner, Berto Paglia. Italian born Chef Paglia developed his love of cooking by assisting his older brother in different restaurants in Venice. After graduating from culinary school in Venice, he apprenticed in some of Italy's top kitchens. After moving to the United States and working in Georgia, Chef Paglia relocated to Aspen to help the Giordanis open Campo in 1994. His personal style of cooking is traditional Italian, with an emphasis on utilizing fresh, local and seasonal ingredients. Elizabeth Giordani rounds out the team by using her talents in marketing and advertising to oversee the presentation, décor, and service etiquette in the front of the house.

The Giordani/Paglia team has taken their very successful formula for Campo de Fiori and has opened restaurants in both Vail and Denver, which bear the same name. They have also opened another Aspen restaurant, Gusto, which also features fine Italian food.

Carpaccio di Bue (Beef Carpaccio)

Ingredients

10 ounces beef tenderloin, very lean
2 tablespoons olive oil
½ lemon
salt and pepper
2 handfuls arugula
2 ounces Parmesan cheese, shaved

Preparation

THINLY slice the beef tenderloin and then place it between plastic wrap and pound it with a meat hammer until very thin. In a bowl, mix the olive oil, a squeeze of fresh lemon, a pinch of salt, and a pinch of pepper, and toss this mixture with the arugula. To serve, layer the slices of tenderloin on 2 plates. Place a handful of the dressed arugula on top of the tenderloin and shave some Parmesan cheese on top of it.

Serves 2

Wine suggestion: Chianti Classico

Salsa alle Erbe Fini

This is a steak or white fish herb sauce, suitable for either grilled or roasted recipes.

Ingredients

2 tablespoons fresh rosemary
2 tablespoons fresh thyme
2 tablespoons fresh sage
2 tablespoons fresh marjoram
1 clove fresh garlic
½ cup extra virgin olive oil
salt and pepper

Preparation

FINELY chop the rosemary, thyme, sage, marjoram, and garlic. Combine in a bowl with the olive oil, a pinch of salt, and a pinch of pepper. Brush onto the cooked meat or fish, or use it as a marinade before cooking.

Wine suggestion: with steak, serve a Napa Valley Cabernet Sauvignon, and with fish or chicken, serve a Chardonnay.

Insalata Pazza

(Spinach Salad with warm dressing)

Ingredients

- *2 tablespoons vegetable oil*
- *½ red onion, thinly sliced*
- *1 cup balsamic vinegar*
- *2 tablespoons black raisins*
- *2 tablespoons pine nuts*
- *1 tablespoon honey*
- *salt and pepper*
- *4 handfuls fresh baby spinach*
- *2 tablespoons crumbled Gorgonzola or blue cheese*

Preparation

IN A medium sauté pan, combine the vegetable oil, onion, balsamic vinegar, raisins, pine nuts, and honey. Cook over low temperature for about 30 minutes, until reduced. Adjust flavor to taste with salt and pepper at the end.

PLACE the washed baby spinach on plates and slowly pour the warm dressing over it, then top with the crumbled Gorgonzola or blue cheese.

Serves 2

Wine suggestion: Sauvignon Blanc or Soave

Farfalle al Salmone

(Bow-tie noodles with salmon cream sauce)

Ingredients

- *8 ounces bow-tie noodles*
- *3 quarts water*
- *2 tablespoons salt*
- *3 ounces smoked salmon*
- *1 tablespoon butter*
- *½ shallot, julienned*
- *4 pre-cooked and cubed Brussels sprouts*
- *2 tablespoons vodka*
- *1 cup heavy cream*
- *2 tablespoons marinara sauce (in-jar Progresso)*
- *2 tablespoons Parmesan cheese, grated*
- *1 tablespoon fresh parsley, chopped*
- *pepper*

Preparation

BRING the water and salt to a rolling boil in a pot. Add noodles to the water and cook to time specified on the package.

CUT smoked salmon into bite-sized pieces. In a medium saucepan sauté the salmon with the butter, shallot, and Brussels sprouts over medium heat for 3 minutes. Add the vodka and evaporate it. Add the marinara sauce and the heavy cream and reduce for 5 minutes. Drain the pasta and toss it in a bowl with the sauce. Add Parmesan cheese, parsley, and pepper, and serve.

Serves 2

Suggested wine: Terre di Tufi or Gavi

Ski course construction in 1930's Aspen.

Pine Creek Cookhouse

Located 1.5 miles from the ghost town of Ashcroft, CO
970-925-1044
www.pinecreekcookhouse.com
Closed Seasonally – Call to Inquire

Winter Season:
Lunch Daily 11:30am – 1:45pm
Dinner Nightly from 6:30pm
Reservations Required for Winter Dining

Summer Season:
Lunch Daily 12:00pm – 1:30pm
Dinner Nightly 6:00pm – 8:30pm
Sunday Brunch also available

Pine Creek Cookhouse

John Wilcox, Owner
Kurt Boucher, Executive Chef

Ashcroft and the upper Castle Creek Valley surrounding the Pine Creek Cookhouse are a veritable Mecca of recreation opportunity. Today only a ghost town, Ashcroft was founded in 1879 and became one of the more stable communities in the area. In 1880 ninety-seven pioneers organized a Miner's Protective Association and laid out the town site to include 840 lots. The town was a fitting rival to nearby Aspen until the Denver & Rio Grande Railroad chose to go through that town instead of Ashcroft.

The Pine Creek Cookhouse is located about one and a half miles from Ashcroft and is accessible by car in the summer, although many guests hike or cycle up the Castle Creek Road to the cabin. In the winter the road is impassable to autos, and guests are picked up at the King Cabin Nordic Center by horse-drawn sleighs. For the more athletic guests, an option to cross-country ski to the cookhouse is available. Originally built in 1971, the cookhouse at the base of Elk Mountain sits nestled against the trees at the edge of a meadow. A fire destroyed the original structure in the spring of 2003, but a spectacular log cabin made of native Colorado logs was built in its place. Huge log beams support the large dining room, and floor-to-ceiling windows face out onto the meadow soaking in the sunsets over the Elk Mountain Range, Taylor Mountain, and Star Peak. On a warm summer day guests can also enjoy lunch on the sunny deck.

The menu covers the range of produce and naturally raised meats found in the region, with Executive Chef Kurt Boucher's modern French and Asian flares creating exquisite dishes. Chef Boucher began his culinary career in Woonsocket, Rhode Island at the age of 13 in a Mom & Pop diner. He continued to work in restaurants until he finished high school and moved to Aspen with his family. His earliest efforts as a line cook at the Pine Creek Cookhouse augmented his desire to pursue a culinary career, and he enrolled at Johnson and Wales University in Providence, Rhode Island. Upon completion of his culinary training in 1996, he returned to the cookhouse as Sous Chef. Under the watchful eyes of Chef Chrissie Mace and owner John Wilcox, he was made Chef de Cuisine after one year and rose to Executive Chef the following year. Featured in numerous culinary magazines and on nationally syndicated television shows, Chef Boucher can be found most nights on the line, in the window of the cookhouse's exhibition kitchen.

Seared Halibut

with Artichoke Ceviche and Watercress Sauce

Ingredients

- *4 6-ounce pieces of halibut*
- *1 teaspoon butter*
- *1 teaspoon grapeseed oil*
- *salt and pepper to taste*
- *Artichoke Ceviche (recipe follows)*
- *Watercress Sauce (recipe follows)*

Preparation

HEAT the oven to 350 degrees. On medium-high heat, sear the fish on both sides in a pan with the butter and oil, and finish it off in the oven for 15 minutes. Season with salt and pepper to taste. Serve with the Artichoke Ceviche and Watercress Sauce.

Serves 4

For the Artichoke Ceviche

- *10 grilled marinated artichokes*
- *3 ounces lime juice*
- *10 ounces tomato concassé*
- *4 ounces red onion, chopped finely*
- *½ ounce jalapeno, chopped*
- *2 ounces scallions, chopped*
- *2 cloves garlic, chopped finely*
- *2 tablespoons olive oil*
- *1 tablespoon cilantro, chopped*
- *salt and pepper to taste*

MIX all ingredients. Allow to marinate for 2 hours. Adjust the seasoning with salt and pepper.

For the Watercress Sauce

- *2 tablespoons shallots, chopped*
- *2 bunches watercress, chopped*
- *2 cups chicken stock or fish stock*
- *1 tablespoon Dijon mustard*
- *¼ cup parsley, chopped*
- *2 teaspoons garlic, finely chopped*
- *1 cup heavy cream*
- *1 tablespoon butter*
- *salt and pepper to taste*

ON medium heat, sweat the shallots and the watercress. Add the stock, mustard, parsley, garlic, cream, butter, and salt and pepper. Reduce the liquid at a simmer for 45 minutes. Keep warm for service.

Rainbow Trout over Shiitake Salad

with Lobster Spring Roll and Miso Beurre Blanc

Ingredients

- 8 *pieces trout*
- *butter or oil to sauté*
- 4 *baby bok choy, sliced*
- 2 *fennel bulbs, sliced*
- 10 *shiitake mushrooms, sliced*
- ¼ *cup Mirin*
- ¼ *cup sweet chili sauce*
- ¼ *cup sweet soy sauce*
- *Miso Beurre Blanc (recipe follows)*
- *Lobster Spring Rolls (recipe follows)*

Preparation

SAUTÉ the trout in a pan on high heat in butter or oil. In a separate pan, add the bok choy, fennel, mushrooms, Mirin, sweet chili sauce, and sweet soy sauce and cook until wilted. To serve, place a portion of the shiitake salad on each plate. Place the trout on the plate, leaning against the salad and drizzle the Miso Beurre Blanc over the trout. Place a spring roll along side.

Serves 8

For the Miso Beurre Blanc

- 1 *cup white wine*
- 1 *tablespoon shallot, chopped*
- 2 *tablespoons rice wine vinegar*
- 1 *bay leaf*
- 2 *sprigs thyme*
- 1 *tablespoon miso*
- 1 *cup cold butter, cut in chunks*

COMBINE the white wine, shallots, vinegar, bay leaf, thyme, and miso. Bring them to a boil, lower the heat, and whisk in the butter piece by piece. When the butter is incorporated, remove from the heat and reserve for serving.

For the Lobster Spring Rolls

- ¼ *pound lobster meat, cooked*
- ¼ *package daikon sprouts*
- ½ *red bell pepper, julienned*
- ½ *yellow bell pepper, julienned*
- ½ *cucumber, julienned*
- ¼ *carrot, julienned*
- 2 *ounces napa cabbage, chiffonade*
- 8 *basil leaves, chiffonade*
- 12 *cilantro leaves, chopped*
- 8 *spring roll wrappers*
- *oil for deep frying*

MIX the lobster meat, daikon sprouts, red and yellow pepper, cucumber, carrot, cabbage, basil and cilantro. Place one wrapper on the table. Place a scoop of the lobster mix in the wrapper, fold in the ends, and roll it up. Deep fry rolls for 3-5 minutes. Keep warm for service.

Cinnamon Dusted Elk Tenderloin

with Pomegranate Syrup and Potato Pavé

Ingredients

- *1 cup flour*
- *4 eggs, beaten*
- *Saigon cinnamon*
- *4 5-ounce elk tenderloins, trimmed of silver skin*
- *butter or oil to sear*
- *Pomegranate Syrup (recipe follows)*
- *Potato Pave (recipe follows)*

Preparation

PLACE the flour on a sheet pan. Place the eggs on a separate sheet pan, and place the cinnamon on third sheet pan. Dip each elk tenderloin into the flour mixture, then into the egg mixture, then finally dip into the cinnamon. Let stand in the refrigerator for at least 1 hour.

HEAT oven to 375 degrees. Heat a sauté pan on medium high, add oil or butter and sear the elk for 2 minutes. Put in the oven for 5 minutes for rare to medium rare. Serve with the Pomegranate Syrup and Potato Pavé. Beef may be substituted for elk.

Serves 4

For the Pomegranate Syrup

- *1 shallot, chopped*
- *1 tablespoon butter*
- *1 cup pomegranate juice*
- *1 cup mirin*
- *1 cup red wine*
- *1 bay leaf*
- *1 cup game demi-glace*

SWEAT the shallot in butter. Add pomegranate juice, mirin, red wine, bay leaf, and demi-glace and reduce for 45 minutes. Reserve for serving.

For the Potato Pavé

- *¼ cup butter, divided*
- *6 potatoes*
- *salt and pepper to taste*
- *1 large clove garlic, minced*
- *1 large shallot, diced*
- *3 tablespoons fresh herbs such as parsley, rosemary, and thyme*

HEAT oven to 375 degrees. In a small baking pan, grease the bottom of the pan with butter. Slice the potatoes about ¼ inch thick and layer in the pan. Top with salt, pepper, garlic, shallots, fresh herbs, and butter. Keep repeating this method until the potatoes are finished. Top with another pan the same size. Inside the second pan use something such as rocks or beans to weigh down the pan. Cook for 45 minutes to 1 hour.

Jack Daniels Marinated Caribou

with Sweet Potato Lasagna

Wild game is best served rare to medium rare. This is the most I would cook this cut because, with the lack of marbling in the meat, if it is cooked over medium it loses its flavor.

Ingredients

- *½ cup Jack Daniels*
- *¼ cup sweet soy*
- *⅓ cup red wine vinegar*
- *¼ cup mirin*
- *1 teaspoon green Tabasco*
- *1 tablespoon brown sugar*
- *2 shallots, chopped*
- *3 pieces garlic, sliced*
- *2 teaspoons pickled ginger, chopped rough*
- *4 6-ounce pieces caribou*
- *Sweet Potato Lasagne (recipe follows)*

Preparation

COMBINE all the ingredients except the caribou and mix well. Add the caribou to the marinade and let it sit for at least 2 hours, but no more than 24 hours.

GRILL the caribou on high heat for 3 minutes on each side for rare, 5 minutes for medium rare. Let stand for at least 2 minutes before you serve it. Serve with Sweet Potato Lasagne and your choice of sautéed greens.

Serves 4

For the Sweet Potato Lasagne

- *4 pounds sweet potatoes, peeled*
- *1 pound clarified butter*
- *salt and pepper to taste*

HEAT oven to 400 degrees. With a mandolin, slice the potatoes into very thin rounds and dry the potatoes. Starting from the center of the pan, overlapping slightly, place the slices in a spiral going clock-wise. Repeat another spiral counter clock-wise. Sprinkle with salt and pepper. Drizzle with the clarified butter, and repeat the process until the pan is filled 2 inches high. Place it in the oven for 20 minutes. Test the center of the lasagna for tenderness. Remove from the pan and drain onto a paper towel.

Soupçon

127-A Elk Avenue
Crested Butte, CO 81224
970-349-5448
www.soupconrestaurant.com

Open Seasonally
Thanksgiving through week in April
June through October
Seatings:
Nightly at 6:00pm and 8:15pm
Reservations Highly Recommended

Soupçon

Scott Green, Chef/Owner

Crested Butte has a lot to offer in spectacular mountain scenery and recreational opportunities. Named a National Historic District, the beautiful downtown area is replete with well-preserved historic buildings and a real sense of a "Western" town. The economy of Crested Butte relies heavily on the tourism industry with great skiing, fly fishing, hunting, mountain biking, hiking, and wildflower viewing. All this activity in the fresh mountain air can work up a strong appetite, and Soupçon is the perfect place to indulge in an intimate dinner cooked to perfection by Chef Scott Greene.

It's easy to miss this place. Tucked in an alley, Soupçon is housed in a charming little rustic log cabin that sports crocheted lace curtains and cheery red flower boxes hanging from the red-trimmed windows. The Kochevar family, who still owns it, built the cabin in 1917. The interior sports rooms with whitewashed walls and floral wallpaper, with tables covered with white linen. Seating at most of the tables is on bentwood chairs, with comfortable wooden benches along the walls. Wine posters and colorful paintings give the rooms the feeling of a French country cabin, the perfect atmosphere to enjoy the French/American cuisine proffered by Proprietor and Chef, Scott Greene.

Growing up in Long Island, New York, Scott was exposed to a wide range of cultures and cuisines at an early age, with grandmothers that came from Greece and Russia. However, cooking as a profession came about by accident. As Scott grew older, he was in need of extra cash for new hockey skates and skis. So he started to work in a restaurant for a few days after school and on weekends. The hustle and bustle of a busy restaurant quickly got under his skin and he knew one day he wanted to have his own establishment. He attended Johnson and Wales University in Providence, Rhode Island and interned and worked in some of the top kitchens throughout the country before settling in Crested Butte. As Scott says, "The life of working in restaurants can be difficult at times, exciting at others. Every day is different than the day before; it brings new challenges and, with that, new goals. This is what keeps me coming back for more. Hopefully you'll keep coming back as well."

Seared Hudson Valley Foie Gras

with Roasted Figs and Fig-Port Purée

Ingredients

- *2 2-ounce slices foie gras*
- *kosher salt and cracked pepper to taste*
- *6 figs, split in half*
- *fleur de sel to taste*
- *Fig-Port Purée (recipe follows)*

Preparation

LIGHTLY score the foie gras and season with salt and pepper. Heat a heavy gauge pan so it is very hot. Place the foie gras in the pan, scored side down. Lower the heat slightly and add the sliced figs. Flip the foie gras over, and cook 1 minute more.

TO SERVE, lay the Fig-Port Purée on the plate, place the figs on top, and the foie gras on the figs. Sprinkle with fleur de sel and enjoy.

Serves 2

Wine suggestion: Sauternes

For the Fig-Port Purée

- *2 cups port wine*
- *15 figs, quartered*

COOK the figs in the port slowly for 25-30 minutes and then purée in a blender. Strain, season, and cool for serving.

Pan-seared Atlantic Halibut

with White Asparagus and Morel Mushrooms

I like to serve this in late spring into early summer when the morels are really great.

Ingredients

8 *white asparagus*
2 *5-ounce halibut filets*
olive oil to sauté
butter to sauté
10 *morel mushrooms*
fleur de sel to taste
2 *teaspoons 21-year-old balsamic vinegar*
extra virgin olive oil
chive flowers to garnish

Preparation

CUT the bottom ¼ inch off the asparagus and peel them to the top. Blanch them in boiling water for 2-3 minutes and then keep warm for serving.

SEASON the halibut with salt and pepper. Sauté the halibut skin side up in olive oil for 3-4 minutes, turn over, cover, and let it finish cooking off the heat for about 4 minutes.

WASH the mushrooms in several changes of water and cut them in half. Sauté them in a little oil and butter until tender. Season and add 1 teaspoon of water to plate.

TO SERVE, lay the asparagus in the center of the plate, and place the mushrooms around the asparagus. Place the halibut on top and drizzle the balsamic and extra virgin olive oil around the plate. Garnish with chive flowers and fleur de sel.

Serves 2

Wine suggestion: Talbot Chardonnay

Maple Leaf Farm Duckling

with Rock Shrimp Hash and Plum Ginger Lacquer

Ingredients

3 *Maple Leaf Farm Ducklings, halved*
Plum Ginger Lacquer (recipe follows)
Rock Shrimp Hash (recipe follows)
Micro greens or scallion greens, to garnish

Preparation

HEAT oven to 475 degrees. Split duckling halves into two pieces (breast and thigh) and roast them, skin-side up for 15-20 minutes.

TO SERVE, transfer the Rock Shrimp Hash to 6 white plates or bowls. Mound it in the center of the dish, and top with two pieces of crisp duckling, breast and thigh, with breast on top. Sauce each duck with Plum Ginger Lacquer and garnish with micro greens or sliced scallion greens.

Serves 6

For the Plum Ginger Lacquer

- 1 *cup soy sauce*
- 1½ *cups plum sauce*
- ½ *cup water*
- 2 *limes, juice from*
- 2 *tablespoons honey*
- 1 *teaspoon sugar*
- 3 *tablespoons ginger, minced*
- 2 *tablespoons garlic, minced*
- 3 *tablespoons corn starch*
- *water, as needed, for corn starch*

IN A saucepot, add the soy sauce, plum sauce, water, limejuice, honey, sugar, ginger, and garlic, and slowly bring to a boil. Thicken slightly with a slurry of corn starch and water. Keep warm for serving.

For the Rock Shrimp Hash

- 2 *russet potatoes, in ½ inch dice*
- 1 *carrot, in ½ inch dice*
- 1 *red pepper, in ½ inch dice*
- 1 *zucchini, in ½ inch dice*
- 1 *yellow squash, in ½ inch dice*
- 12 *shiitake mushrooms, quartered*
- 1 *bunch asparagus, tips only*
- *olive oil to coat vegetables*
- *salt and pepper to taste*
- 30 *rock shrimp, 31-40 per pound*
- 2 *tablespoons olive oil*

HEAT oven to 475 degrees. Using a small amount of olive, toss the vegetables in separate bowls: 1 for the potatoes, 1 for carrot, 1 for red pepper, and 1 for the rest of the vegetables. Season each with salt and pepper. In a heavy pan, roast the potato in the oven. After 5 minutes, add the carrots and roast for approximately 10-12 minutes more, shaking the pan to toss the mixture around and brown the potatoes and carrots. When tender, remove to a new container and keep warm. In the same roasting pan, add the red peppers and cook for 2-3 minutes. Add the zucchini, squash, mushrooms, and asparagus and cook until just tender. Add to the potatoes and carrots.

IN A large sauté pan heat 2 tablespoons olive oil until it is almost smoking, add the shrimp and sauté for 2-3 minutes. Add the vegetables and mix together. Remove from heat and reserve for serving.

Soupçon Crème Brûlée

Ingredients

2 cups heavy whipping cream
4 tablespoons turbinado sugar
1 vanilla bean, scraped
½ pinch salt
4 egg yolks
turbinado sugar to dust

Preparation

HEAT oven to 340 degrees. Scald the cream with the sugar, vanilla bean, and salt. Beat the egg yolks for 1 minute, temper the cream into yolks, and strain. Divide into 4 ovenproof ramekins, cover with foil, and cook in a water bath in the oven for 30 minutes. Custard should still jiggle a little when done. Cool 1 hour at room temperature, then 3 hours more in the refrigerator. Dust the cold custard with turbinado sugar and dump the excess out. Burn the sugar with a torch or under the broiler, and let rest 1 minute before serving.

Serves 4

Wine suggestion: Moscato di Asti, lightly sparkling

Cazwellas

foods of the americas
CAZWELLAS
Montrose, Colorado

320 E. Main
Montrose, CO 81401
970-252-9200
www.cazwellas.com

Dinner:
Monday thru Saturday 5:00 to 9:00pm

Cazwellas

Keithley Wagner, Co-Owner
Donn Wagner, Executive Chef/Co-Owner

Donn and Keithley Wagner originally opened Cazwellas in Telluride but, after four years, decided that they wanted a restaurant that would be open year round. After searching from coast to coast, they ended up not far from their original venture. In the fall of 2001 they fell in love with the building that had housed the old Stockmen's Café & Bar on historic Main Street in Montrose. In 1892, W.S. Callaway opened The Pastime as a gentlemen's resort but, for over fifty years, the Stockmen's Café & Bar occupied the space. The old Stockmen's was home to many sheep herders and cattlemen, as well as movie stars like John Wayne and Glenn Campbell who bellied up to the bar.

Donn and Keithley spent six months renovating the structure and bringing it close to its original façade. The original fir floors are now exposed as are the old brick walls and tin ceiling that is in the completely renovated state-of-the-art kitchen. Before opening Cazwellas in 2002, the couple took an extended trip to the Oaxaca region of Mexico to immerse them in the local cooking that became the signature of their restaurant. Here, Donn worked with the local women who made a special Mole Negro that is now part of the restaurant's signature dish, Hen with Mole Negro. The recipe is extremely complicated and takes three days to make, but Donn feels it is well worth the effort as he sees the pleasure-filled faces of his guests when he serves it.

Donn's culinary philosophy is to serve the food of the Americas, both north and south, and to emphasize fresh and flavor-enhancing moles and salsas. Donn tries to buy only organic and pesticide-free meats, poultry, fish, and vegetables as the foundation for his recipes. To accompany the food selections, Donn and Keithley have acquired an extensive list of wines, as well as over 65 different kinds of tequila. The wine list quickly came to the attention of the *Wine Spectator*, and it has won the Award of Excellence every year since 2004, making Cazwellas the first restaurant in Montrose to achieve this distinction.

The dining room is light and airy, with its high ceiling and exposed brick walls. Rich burgundy leather banquettes line the walls and a shoulder mount of a Texas longhorn steer dominates the partition wall in the center of the restaurant, tying the history of the place. The atmosphere is lively and friendly, with locals and tourists chatting freely.

Award of Excellence

Jicama Salsa

This light tasting salsa is a great alternative to the traditional pico de gallo. We use it to garnish fish, poultry, and even the Grilled Pork Chop with Mole Manchamantel.

Ingredients

- *1 1-pound jicama*
- *2 Granny Smith apples*
- *4 radishes*
- *½ red onion*
- *2 ounces fresh orange juice*
- *1 orange, zest from*
- *2 ounces red wine vinegar*
- *1 tablespoon extra virgin olive oil*

Preparation

PEEL and fine dice the jicama, apples, radishes, and red onion. Combine with the orange juice, orange zest, and red wine vinegar. When all ingredients are tossed together, add 1 tablespoon of extra virgin olive oil. This salsa will keep two days when covered and refrigerated.

Serves 20

Grilled Pork Chop
with Mole Manchamantel

We use this mole (pronounced molay) for our frenched double-cut 14-ounce pork chop. This mole is very full of flavor with a nice spice on the finish. Manchamantel translates to "stain the tablecloth", so be careful!

Ingredients

- *5 ancho chilies, seeded*
- *2 chili guajillo, seeded*
- *1½ cups pineapple juice*
- *1 Roma tomato, roasted*
- *1 clove garlic, roasted*
- *¾ cup pineapple, peeled and cored*
- *1 ripe plantain*
- *½ Granny Smith apple*
- *½ teaspoon ground cinnamon*
- *1 tablespoon apple cider vinegar*
- *⅛ teaspoon ground cloves*
- *½ teaspoon salt*
- *2 teaspoons dark brown sugar*
- *1 tablespoon canola oil*
- *2 pork chops*

Preparation

SEED and remove stems from chilies. Add pineapple juice and chilies to a saucepan and warm until chilies are soft. Coarse chop the roasted tomato, garlic, pineapple, plantain, and apple. Put them in a blender with the cinnamon, apple cider vinegar, ground cloves, salt, and brown sugar. Purée until very smooth.

IN A large roasting pan, preferably cast iron, heat the canola oil until light smoke appears. Pour mole into pan. Be very careful at this point. It will splatter! You are basically frying the mole. Reduce heat and simmer for 5 minutes. Allow to cool some, but serve warm. Keep remaining mole covered and refrigerated for up to one week.

GRILL the pork chop to desired doneness. To serve, plate the pork chop over a slice of grilled pineapple and 1 to 2 ounces of Mole Manchamantel.

Serves 2

Beverage suggestions: This combination is excellent with a good Mexican beer, such as Dos Equis Lager. For a lovely white Spanish wine, try Marques de Riscal Rueda. For a lush, velvety Spanish red, try 1998 Hacienda de Monasterio.

Flan

This is the ultimate simple dessert. Make it in four-ounce soufflé cups.

Ingredients

3 cups C&H cane sugar, divided
1 cup half and half
1 cup whole milk
1 four-inch stick of cinnamon (canela)
4 eggs
1 tablespoon Kahlua
½ teaspoon vanilla

Preparation

PLACE 2½ cups cane sugar in a non-stick saucepan over medium heat. Watch carefully. When sugar begins to melt, stir with a non-stick spoon until all sugar is melted and golden brown. Be patient, this takes awhile. Be careful! You now have molten lava in the pan. Very carefully, pour enough in each soufflé cup to cover bottom and ½ inch up the side. Remember, this is very hot stuff and will burn you. Pay attention. Do not try to taste or touch the liquid sugar. Let cups cool for 30 minutes before filling with egg mixture.

IN A saucepan, heat the half and half, whole milk, and cinnamon together and scald. Remove from heat and add the remaining ½ cup sugar. Stir until dissolved. It is very important not to add sugar before this point. This way you will have a much smoother flan when you finish.

IN A separate mixing bowl, combine eggs, Kahlua, and vanilla. Beat until blended. Do not over beat. Air bubbles and froth are the enemy. Temper warm milk mixture into the eggs. Stir until combined. Pour through a fine chinois. Add custard mixture to cooled soufflé cups.

HEAT oven to 350 degrees. Place soufflé cups in an oven proof pan. Fill pan with water half way up the outer sides of the cups. Cover pan with foil and place in center of 350-degree oven for 20-25 minutes. Check in 20 minutes. As soon as the flan begins to set, remove pan from oven and leave covered. The flan will finish cooking.

TO SERVE, place pan with water on stovetop. Bring to a simmer. Place soufflé cup in hot water for 1 - 2 minutes. Run an offset palette knife around edge of cup to loosen flan. Place serving plate over the top of the cup and invert. Jiggle inverted cup and remove. You should be looking at the top of a beautiful, simple dessert covered with melted caramelized sugar. Enjoy!

Serves 5

Cowboys at lunch ca 1940.

Remington's

REMINGTON'S
· AT THE BRIDGES ·

Golf and Country Club
2500 Bridges Drive
Montrose, CO 81402
970-252-8899

Lunch & Dinner:
Tuesday thru Sunday [hours?]
Sunday Brunch [hours?]

Remington's

Thomas Blassingame, Executive Chef
David Koffman, Executive Sous Chef

Remington's at The Bridges Golf and Country Club is named for Frederic Remington, a prominent 18th century painter, sculptor, illustrator, and writer. He dramatized the old West with his renderings of horses, Native Americans, soldiers, and cowboys, and struck a chord with the American public's idealization of the western lifestyle. One of Remington's bronzes, *The Buffalo Signal*, is also on display in the restaurant.

Thomas Blassingame recently joined The Bridges as Executive Chef, with nine years of experience in country club and resort settings under his belt. Thomas' formal culinary training in Austin, Texas prepared him to serve admirably in restaurants across the nation, from South Carolina to Texas. He and his fiancée, Kelly, moved from Texas to Montrose in 2005 to fulfill their dream of living in the mountains of Colorado. Most recently, Thomas worked as one of three chefs at Tarragon at Elk Mountain Resort. During his time there, Thomas helped in earning the chefs an invitation to the renowned James Beard House in New York. As a Texas boy, Thomas favors the grill, but is also very skilled in the more refined culinary arts. Thomas Keller and Auguste Escoffier are his culinary heroes. His influences span the globe, and include Southwest, French, Cajun, Asian, Italian, and good ol' Texas barbeque. Thomas' upbeat, positive attitude creates an enjoyable atmosphere for members and employees alike. Just don't be surprised if you hear singing coming from the kitchen!

Executive Sous Chef, David Koffman, spent eleven years working in the hotels of Las Vegas, Nevada, including five years at The Mirage. He was invited to join the staff at Tarragon at Elk Mountain Resort, where he met Chef Thomas. He has visited the southwest Colorado area for many years on vacation and was attracted to the area by its abundance of outdoor activities. He also manages to serve the community of Montrose as a volunteer firefighter and EMT.

Remington's continues the classic idea of preserving the historical beauty of the west, while at the same time providing an oasis of casual elegance to its visitors. The organic and locally produced menu items reflect a fundamental belief in appreciating nature and the natural bounty of the land in the Montrose area. The stunning views of the San Juan Mountain Range and the Uncompahgre Valley from the dining area remind us that the beauty of the west remains as breathtaking and awesome as it was in Frederic Remington's time.

Butternut Squash Soup

with Spring Vegetable & Chorizo Beggar's Purse

Ingredients

- *1 pound butternut squash, pared, seeded, and cut into 1-inch cubes*
- *2 cups chicken broth*
- *½ cup whipping cream*
- *¼ cup white wine*
- *¼ teaspoon salt*
- *¼ teaspoon white pepper*
- *Spring Vegetable and Chorizo Beggar's Purse (recipe follows)*

Preparation

PLACE the squash cubes into the chicken broth and bring to a boil. Reduce the heat and let it simmer for 10 minutes. Turn off the heat and let steep until fork tender. Cool and place it in a food processor. Blend into a purée. Return the squash purée to low heat, and add cream and white wine. Simmer slowly another 5 minutes. Add salt and pepper to taste.

HEAT oven to 350 degrees. To serve, warm the filled Beggar's Purses in the oven for 3 minutes. Place in the center of a large soup bowl, pour the soup around the Beggar's Purses, and serve immediately.

Serves 4

For the Spring Vegetable & Chorizo Beggar's Purse

- *1 cup all purpose flour, sifted*
- *3 tablespoons unsalted butter, browned*
- *1 egg*
- *1 pinch salt*
- *½ cup milk*
- *¼ cup zucchini, small diced*
- *¼ cup yellow squash, small diced*
- *¼ cup red bell pepper, small diced*
- *1 shallot, minced*
- *1 tablespoon fresh basil, chiffonade*
- *¼ cup chorizo, small diced*
- *4 large chives, whole*

WHIP together the flour, butter, egg, salt, and milk for crepe batter. The batter should be thin. Let it stand for 1 hour.

HEAT an 8-inch non-stick pan to medium. Spray with non-stick spray. Pour 1 ounce of the batter into the pan and swirl the pan, tipping front to back and side to side. Allow the batter to cover the entire bottom of the pan. Cook until the crepe pulls free of the sides of the pan, about 1-2 minutes. Delicately flip the crepe to the opposite side and finish cooking, about 25 seconds. Place the crepe on a plate to cool. Layer the crepes with parchment paper in between them.

IN A heated sauté pan, add the zucchini, yellow squash, bell pepper, shallot, basil, and chorizo and sweat. Let cool, then place a portion of the vegetable and chorizo mix in the center of each crepe. Fold the crepe up in half to form a half moon, and then bring the corners in to the middle like a Chinese dumpling. Tie off with a chive.

French Bean Salad

with Tomato Tartar and Chive Oil

Be sure to read recipe through before preparing. The Chive Oil needs to sit overnight before using.

Ingredients

- *2 tablespoons kosher salt*
- *1 pound French beans, cleaned*
- *2 tablespoons red wine vinegar*
- *2 large shallots, diced*
- *1 cup whipping cream*
- *3 slices applewood smoked bacon, cooked & chopped*
- *1 pinch freshly ground black pepper*
- *1 pinch salt*
- *2 slices applewood smoked bacon, cooked & sliced on bias*
- *½ cup pine nuts, toasted*
- *Chive Oil (recipe follows)*
- *Tomato Tartar (recipe follows)*

Preparation

BRING 2 quarts of water to a boil. Add the salt and the beans and boil for about 3-4 minutes. They should still have a snap but be cooked. Place them in an ice water bath to cool quickly. When they have completely cooled, drain and set aside.

IN A mixing bowl, combine the vinegar, shallots, cream, chopped bacon, and a pinch of salt and pepper. Whip until soft peaks develop. Fold in the beans and set aside.

TO SERVE, use a 3-inch ring mold, and lightly drizzle the Chive Oil in the center. Layer the Tomato Tartar over the oil in the ring mold to about ¼ inch tall. Pull up the ring mold and the Chive Oil should run. Next, place the marinated beans atop the Tomato Tartar, layering them four beans at a time, each layer at a 90-degree angle to the one below. Garnish with the sliced bacon on either side of the stack of beans. Sprinkle with pine nuts, and serve.

Serves 4

For the Chive Oil

- *¼ pound chives*
- *½ cup salad oil*
- *½ cup extra virgin olive oil*

BRING 1 quart of water to a boil and add the chives. Turn off the heat, allowing the chives to steep for about 1 minute. Drain the chives, and place them in an ice water bath to cool. Drain thoroughly, trying to remove as much water as possible. Put the cooled, drained, chives, salad oil, and olive oil in a blender and blend for 1 minute. Pour this mixture into a mixing bowl and leave out at room temperature overnight. The next day, strain it through a fine strainer to remove the chives. The remaining oil should be a bright green. Reserve at room temperature for use.

For the Tomato Tartar

- 2 *medium roma tomatoes*
- 2 *medium yellow tomatoes*
- 3 *cloves garlic, diced*
- 1 *tablespoon fresh basil, chopped*
- 1 *tablespoon thyme, chopped*
- ¼ *teaspoon freshly ground pepper*
- 1 *pinch kosher salt*
- ½ *cup extra virgin olive oil*

HEAT oven to 225 degrees. Halve and deseed the tomatoes. Place them in a mixing bowl and toss with the garlic, basil, thyme, pepper, salt, and olive oil. Lay the tomatoes on a wire rack over a cookie tray. Pour the oil mix left in the bowl over the tomatoes. Place the tomatoes in the oven and cook for 3 hours. Tomatoes should dry out but not burn. When the tomatoes are done, let them cool at room temperature for about 1 hour. Then place them in a container with a small amount of olive oil and refrigerate. Rough chop the tomatoes for serving.

Rock Shrimp and Brie Stuffed Halibut

with Sun-dried Tomato Pesto Butter, Almond Rice Pilaf, Wilted Spinach, and Candied Lemon

Ingredients

- 1 *tablespoon garlic, minced*
- 3 *tablespoons butter*
- 1 *pound shrimp, diced small*
- ½ *pound Brie, crumbled*
- 2 *cups breadcrumbs*
- ½ *teaspoon thyme*
- ½ *teaspoon oregano*
- *salt and pepper to taste*
- 4 *halibut filets, 6-8 ounce portions*
- *Almond Rice Pilaf (recipe follows)*
- *Sun-dried Tomato Pesto Butter (recipe follows)*
- *Candied Lemon (recipe follows)*
- *Wilted Spinach (recipe follows)*

Preparation

SAUTÉ the garlic in the butter until lightly browned. Add the diced shrimp and sauté until fully cooked. Transfer to a mixing bowl and add the Brie cheese, breadcrumbs, thyme, and oregano and mix together into a stuffing. Add salt and pepper to taste.

HEAT the oven to 375 degrees. Slice the halibut filets in half, leaving one edge as a hinge (butterfly cut). Place the stuffing inside of the halibut and fold over. Season with salt and pepper and place the stuffed halibut in the oven. Halibut should take 15 minutes to cook.

TO SERVE, place the Almond Rice Pilaf on dinner plates and place the halibut filets on the rice. Pour the Sun-dried Tomato Pesto Butter over the fish and top with Candied Lemon. Serve the Wilted Spinach on the side. (continued)

Serves 4

Rock Shrimp and Brie Stuffed Halibut, continued

For the Almond Rice Pilaf

½ cup carrot, diced small
½ cup celery, diced small
butter to sauté
3 cups jasmine rice
½ cup green onion, chopped
½ cup almonds, toasted
salt and pepper to taste

SAUTÉ the carrot and celery in butter until tender. Add jasmine rice and sauté until slightly browned, stirring frequently. Add water until covered and cook over low heat until done. Add chopped green onion and toasted almonds after the rice is cooked. Add salt and pepper to taste and reserve for serving.

For the Sun-dried Tomato Pesto Butter

8 ounces sun-dried tomato pesto
2 tablespoons butter

WARM up the sun-dried tomato pesto and fold in the butter to make a slightly thinner sauce. Reserve for serving.

For the Candied Lemon

1 cup water
1 cup sugar
1 lemon, sliced ⅛ inch thick

MIX the sugar and water in a small saucepan. Add the sliced lemon and bring to a boil. Remove from the heat, drain the sugar water, and let the slices cool to room temperature.

For the Wilted Spinach

1 tablespoon garlic, chopped
2 pounds baby spinach leaves
½ cup white wine

PLACE a large sauté pan on high heat. Add the chopped garlic and stir quickly to prevent burning. Add the spinach and wine and stir quickly until wilted.

GRILLED FILET MIGNON

with Roasted Jalapeno Béarnaise, Gorgonzola Mashers, and Baked Tomato Spinach Mousse

Ingredients

- 2 tablespoons chili powder
- 1 tablespoon kosher salt
- 1 tablespoon freshly ground black pepper
- ½ tablespoon granulated garlic
- ½ tablespoon granulated onion
- ½ tablespoon dried thyme
- ½ tablespoon dried basil
- ½ tablespoon dried oregano
- 1 tablespoon extra virgin olive oil
- 4 8-ounce beef tenderloins, trimmed and well marbled
- Roasted Jalapeno Béarnaise (recipe follows)
- Gorgonzola Mashers (recipe follows)
- Baked Tomato Spinach Mousse (recipe follows)

Preparation

COMBINE the chili powder, salt, pepper, garlic, onion, thyme, basil, and oregano. Two hours before grilling lightly oil the steaks and generously apply the seasoning mixture to all sides of the steaks. Grill the steaks at high heat to desired doneness, medium rare is recommended.

TO SERVE, ladle some of the Roasted Jalapeno Béarnaise on 4 dinner plates. Place a grilled steak on the sauce, and surround with the Gorgonzola Mashers and the Tomato Spinach Mousse.

Serves 4

For the Roasted Jalapeno Béarnaise

- 2 jalapenos
- 5 egg yolks
- ½ lemon, juice from
- salt and pepper to taste
- 4 ounces clarified butter
- 2 tablespoons dried tarragon
- ½ cup red wine
- 1 shallot, minced

ROAST the jalapeno, peel the skin, and remove the seeds and veins. Set aside. Set up a double boiler or saucepan half full with water. Bring to a boil and then reduce heat to medium. Place the egg yolks, lemon juice, salt, and pepper in a large metal mixing bowl. Hold the bowl over the pan of boiling water, whisking quickly. Be careful to only hold the bowl over the pan for a short period of time so as not to scramble the yolks. Whisk until lemon yellow in color. In another saucepan, melt the butter on low heat being careful NOT TO BOIL! Skim the white film from the top of the melted butter. Slowly whisk the butter into the egg yolks. Pour the tarragon, red wine, and shallots into a saucepan and reduce on high heat until almost dry. Add this to the egg sauce. Dice the roasted jalapeno, and add to the sauce. Reserve for serving. (continued)

Grilled Filet Mignon, continued

For the Gorgonzola Mashers

- 3 *Idaho potatoes, peeled & diced*
- ¾ *cup milk*
- 3 *ounces unsalted butter*
- 1 *tablespoon kosher salt*
- 2 *ounces Gorgonzola cheese*

IN A large pot, cover the potatoes with cold water and bring to a boil. Reduce heat and simmer. Cook the potatoes until fork tender and drain all the water out. Whip the potatoes with a heavy whisk. While continuing to whisk, add the rest of the ingredients and whip until fluffy.

For the Baked Tomato Spinach Mousse

- 1 *pound fresh tomatoes, cut in half and deseeded*
- 2 *tablespoons shallot, minced*
- 1 *tablespoon garlic, minced*
- 2 *ounces unsalted butter*
- ¼ *cup white wine*
- 1 *pound fresh spinach, chopped*
- 1 *cup heavy cream*
- 2 *tablespoons Parmesan cheese*
- 1 *egg white*
- ½ *tablespoon kosher salt*
- ¼ *tablespoon fresh ground black pepper*

HEAT oven to 325 degrees. Caramelize the shallots in butter. Add the garlic and deglaze with white wine. Add chopped spinach and sweat all moisture out of the spinach. Add the cream, salt, and pepper and reduce by half. Cool in the refrigerator. After cooling, froth egg white to a soft peak and fold into mixture with Parmesan. Scoop mixture into cleaned tomato halves and bake for 10 minutes in 325-degree oven.

Ginger Wild Blueberry Sorbet

Ingredients

- *1½ cups frozen wild blueberries*
- *1 cup sugar*
- *½ cup water*
- *1 tablespoon blackberry liqueur*
- *2 tablespoons lime juice (half a lime)*
- *1 egg white*
- *1 cup fresh wild blueberries, plus extra for garnish*
- *4 mint leaves*

Preparation

PLACE an 8-inch sauté pan on the burner, turn the burner to medium high heat, and heat the pan. When the pan is hot, add the blueberries, and sear for 1 minute to extract the sugar from the berry. Next add the sugar, water, liqueur, and limejuice and simmer for 2 minutes. Remove from the heat, place in a bowl, and cool in the refrigerator.

WHIP the egg white until soft peaks develop and set aside. When the berry mixture has cooled completely, fold in the egg white. Place this mixture in the freezer, and stir every 10 minutes until ice crystals begin to appear. Cover, and leave it in the freezer to harden.

TO SERVE, scoop one ounce of the sorbet into a small serving glass, sprinkle with fresh berries, and garnish with a mint leaf.

Serves 4

Prospecting party eating by the Dolores River in 1908.

Tarragon at Elk Mountain Resort

Richard Chamberlain, Consulting Culinary Director
Paul A. Venturo, Executive Chef

The luxury and beauty surrounding the 275-acre Elk Mountain Resort has earned it a *Condé Nast Johansens Award* for 2006 as "Most Excellent Resort in the USA". Surrounded by pristine national forests and the San Juan Mountains, a guest at the resort is treated to all the best of outdoor activities available in southwestern Colorado, including a state-of-the-art shooting club. In the center of this property sits a spectacular structure built on the concept of a 19th century hunting lodge. Walk through the front doors into a lobby of massive wood and stone, with plush leather chairs surrounding a majestic fireplace.

As you turn left from the lobby you come upon the chic dining room that is Tarragon. Walk through the glass-paned French doors and enter an elegant room dominated by a massive stone fireplace and featuring a beautiful lightly stained wood floor that contrasts with the dark wood tables and high-backed leather chairs. When the weather is conducive, guests can also dine on the lovely patio accessed from the dining room. Comfortable teak chairs and tables with umbrellas are scattered across the patio, which features a grand three-sided fireplace and a delightful view across the picturesque lake.

Tarragon features Alpine Pyrenee as well as regional cuisine originally conceived by the Consulting Culinary Director, Richard Chamberlain. Chamberlain is the recipient of many national awards. Early in his career, he was selected as one of 1988's *Rising Stars to Watch* by *Food & Wine Magazine*. In 1992, he was nominated for *The Best Chef of the Northwest Award* by the James Beard Foundation. During his career, he has served as Executive Chef at Ratcliff's in Dallas, Executive Sous Chef at Hotel Bel-Air in Los Angeles, Executive Sous Chef under Dean Fearing at the Mansion at Turtle Creek in Dallas, and Executive Chef at the Little Nell in Aspen. He currently is the Chef/Proprietor of both Chamberlain's Steak and Chop House and Chamberlain's Fish Market Grill.

Adjacent to Tarragon and down a hand-carved trail is the 2,500-bottle Wine Cellar with a state-of-the-art climate control system. Designed to look like an authentic mine shaft, the cellar features a grand tasting room which can be used for a private dining room. Almost from its inception, Tarragon has been honored with the *Wine Spectator's Award of Excellence* each year.

Award of Excellence

Duck Cakes

Ingredients

2 pounds duck confit, picked
1 cup red bell pepper, diced
3 shallots, peeled, chopped
1 cup Japanese bread crumbs
6 egg yolks
salt and pepper to taste

Preparation

IN A large mixing bowl, combine all ingredients and mix well, making sure that the cakes will bind together. Form into 3-ounce cakes and place on a sheet pan lined with parchment paper. To store for later use, individually wrap the cakes in parchment and wrap them in plastic wrap and keep in refrigerator or freezer.

TO SERVE, sear the cakes in a sauté pan over medium high heat until done.

Yield: 10 cakes

Wine suggestions: Chablis Chardonnay from France, creamy but still light and crisp

Mer Soleil Chardonnay from California, bigger body, much more extracted with a long finish

Gloria Ferrer Pinot Noir from California, light, fruity, with a touch of spice

Mushroom Onion Soup

Ingredients

6 yellow onions, julienned
grapeseed oil, to sauté
2 ounces garlic, chopped
1 cup dry sherry
2 quarts remouillage, or chicken stock
2 quarts mushroom stock
1 sachet of sage and thyme
kosher salt and pepper to taste
dark soy sauce to taste

Preparation

CARMELIZE the onions in a large rondeau with grapeseed oil. Add the garlic and cook for about 30 seconds. Deglaze with sherry. Add the remouillage and mushroom stock. Add the sachet and let it simmer for 1 hour. Season with salt and pepper and soy sauce until proper taste is reached. Remove from heat and serve.

Serves 6 quarts

Wine suggestion: Gogondas Syrah from France's Rhone valley, full-bodied, robust, earthy, spicy kick

Elk Mountain Mushroom Mix

This is a delicious mushroom mix that is frequently used in the restaurant. You can make it at home in smaller quantities, using equal parts of several different mushrooms. This mix is used in the Pheasant Crepe recipe.

Ingredients

black trumpet mushrooms
chanterelle yellowfoot mushrooms
oyster mushrooms
trumpet royale mushrooms
wood ear mushrooms
grapeseed oil
5 *tablespoons garlic, peeled and minced*
5 *sprigs fresh rosemary*
salt and pepper to taste
mushroom stock

Preparation

CLEAN all mushrooms. Put on a sheet tray with paper towels overnight to dry. Trim all stems and discard or save for stock. Slice the mushrooms 1/8 inch thick. Heat rondeau to medium to high heat, depending on the moisture content of the mushrooms. Add the grapeseed oil. Sauté the trumpet mushrooms without overcrowding the pan. When mushrooms have some color, add 1 tablespoon garlic and 1 sprig rosemary broken in 2 pieces, and season with salt and pepper. Deglaze with mushroom stock. Remove from heat, place mushrooms on a sheet pan with parchment paper. Place on speed rack to cool. Clean the rondeau and repeat the cooking process with each type of mushrooms separately. When all mushrooms are cooked and cooled, remove the rosemary and combine well in a mixing bowl. Place into a suitable sized container and reserve for use.

Duck Confit

Ingredients

6 spanish onions, julienned
20 cloves peeled garlic
4 ounces parsley
4 ounces fresh sage
4 ounces fresh rosemary
4 ounces fresh thyme
24 drake Muscovy duck legs, bone-in
kosher salt and ground black pepper to taste
duck fat

Preparation

LINE the bottom of a 6-inch hotel pan with a layer of julienned onion, 10 cloves of garlic, and some of the parsley, sage, rosemary, and thyme. Season the duck legs thoroughly with salt and pepper. Place them in the pan snugly against one another and then layer more of the onion, garlic, and herbs over the top. Continue until all the legs are seasoned and layered with the onion, garlic, and herbs. Place a sheet of plastic wrap directly on top of the legs. Place another pan over the duck legs and weigh it down with cans (tomato sauce, jelly, etc) so there is no space between the top pan and the duck. Let the duck cure in the refrigerator for 48 hours.

HEAT the oven to 200 degrees. In a rondeau, sear the duck legs, sealing them to hold their juices. Discard the onions, garlic, and herbs used to cure the duck. Melt enough duck fat to cover the legs. Place legs, now covered in fat in the hotel pan. Cover with aluminum foil and place in the oven for at least 6-10 hours, depending on the volume of the duck being cooked. Duck should fall off the bone when lifted from the fat. Let it cool in the refrigerator, letting the duck fat congeal with the legs still in it. This will seal the meat from any air, ensuring the longevity of the meat.

WHEN needed, melt the whole pan with the fat and remove just what you need. Place the pan back in the refrigerator to congeal again. Enjoy!

Yield: 24 legs

Pheasant Crepe

Ingredients

- 1½ *ounces smoked pheasant breast*
- *oil or butter to sauté*
- 1 *teaspoon tomatoes, diced*
- 1 *ounce Mushroom Mix, see recipe in this section*
- ½ *teaspoon hot herbs*
- 1 *ounce Madeira wine*
- 1 *teaspoon port wine*
- 1 *ounce heavy cream*
- *salt and pepper to taste*
- 2 *ounces baby mixed lettuce*
- 1 *teaspoon feta cheese*
- *Sherry Vinaigrette (recipe follows)*

Preparation

DICE the pheasant breast. In a black steel pan sauté the tomatoes and mushroom mix. Add the pheasant and hot herbs and continue to sauté. Deglaze with the Madeira and port wine and reduce until almost dry. Add the cream and season with salt and pepper.

TO SERVE, dress the lettuce with the Sherry Vinaigrette, place pheasant mixture on top, and sprinkle with feta cheese.

Serves 1

Wine suggestions: Sendrio de Cruces Albarino from Spain, high acidity but still full bodied

Meursault Chardonnay from Burgundy, France, bigger and creamy

Marsanay Pinot Noir from Burgundy, France, medium bodied

For the Sherry Vinaigrette

- 1 *cup sherry La Posada vinegar*
- 1 *shallot, diced*
- 2 *tablespoons Dijon mustard*
- 1 *teaspoon thyme, chopped*
- 1½ *cups grape seed oil*
- 1½ *cups extra virgin olive oil*
- *salt and pepper to taste*

COMBINE vinegar, shallot, mustard, and thyme. While whisking, slowly add the oils to mix. Adjust seasoning with salt and pepper.

A man and two boys catching fish and cooking over a fire with a creel and fishing tackle in the foreground circa 1925.

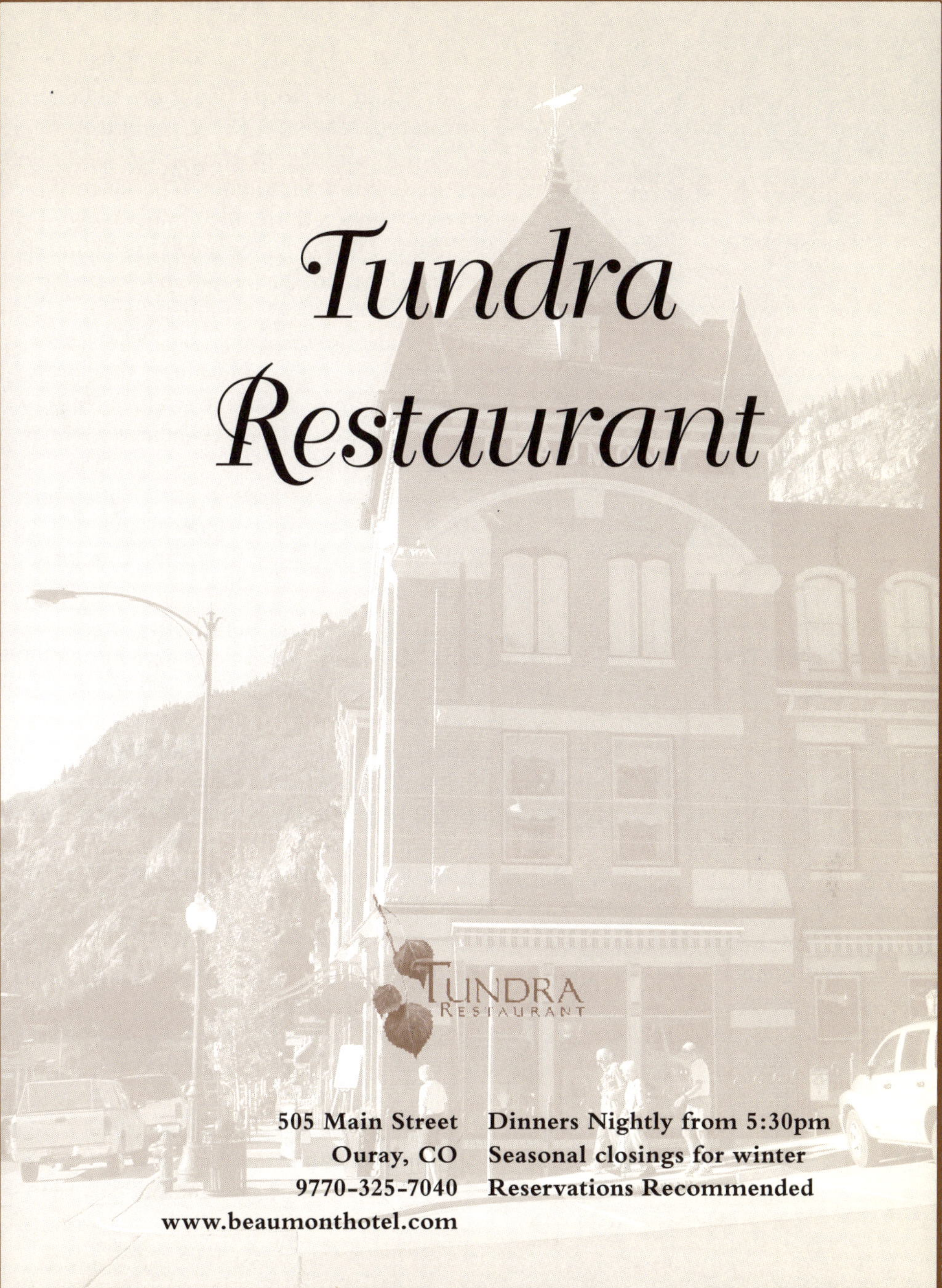
Tundra Restaurant
TUNDRA RESTAURANT
505 Main Street
Ouray, CO
9770-325-7040
www.beaumonthotel.com
Dinners Nightly from 5:30pm
Seasonal closings for winter
Reservations Recommended

Tundra Restaurant

David Weber, Executive Chef

Located on the second floor of the beautifully restored Beaumont Hotel, Tundra Restaurant features an elegant atmosphere and offers a romantic, historic fine dining experience that will long be remembered. In 1875, miners were drawn to the town of Ouray as the news of silver and gold leaked out. By 1886, the Beaumont Hotel was being built in order to attract capitalists to the town to invest in the mining businesses. The hotel soon became known as the "Flagship of the San Juans" and served as the social and political hub of the community. The original hotel had a skylight, grand staircase, and interior balconies that open into the hotel's atrium. It has been reported that some of the hotel's more prominent guests included Theodore Roosevelt, Sarah Bernhardt and King Leopold of Belgium.

The hotel was open for more than eighty years until the mid-1960s, when its owner had a dispute with the city and closed the Beaumont, vowing it would never reopen. Sadly, the building sat empty for over 35 years, becoming a rundown warehouse, and having part of its roof collapse in a snowstorm. The once grand hotel almost met demolition but was saved when new owners purchased the building at auction in 1998. Understanding the historic value of the structure, they poured several million dollars and five years of hard work into renovating it. Much time was spent studying historic documents in order to replicate the original carpeting and wallpaper patterns as well as to restore as many of the original components as possible. This included a full year's work of patiently hand scrubbing each brick on the exterior, as it had been painted pink at some time.

Opened in October 2002, the Tundra Restaurant is in the same location as the original restaurant in the hotel. The restaurant boasts 28-foot ceilings and restored Romanesque stained glass windows that were found in boxes in the hotel. Only open a few years, the restaurant is gaining a fine reputation, including the honor of receiving the *Award of Excellence* from the *Wine Spectator Magazine*. Executive Chef David Weber presides over the kitchen. Graduated from the restaurant school in Pennsylvania in 1994, he has over nine years experience as Sous Chef, working for restaurants including Black Horse Restaurant in Denver, Pennsylvania and the Historic Strasburg Village Inn in Strasburg, Pennsylvania, as well as Pinon Restaurant in Ouray. Chef Weber's goal is to feature locally grown produce and meats, whenever possible and to serve food with a distinctly Colorado flair.

Award of Excellence

Jumbo Lump Crab Cakes over Wilted Spinach

with Champagne Dijon Cream and Roasted Red Pepper Coulis

Ingredients

- *1 egg*
- *1 tablespoon Dijon mustard*
- *½ cup mayonnaise*
- *1 lemon, juice from*
- *1 tablespoon Old Bay*
- *2 splashes Worcestershire sauce*
- *1 tablespoon chives, finely chopped*
- *1 pound jumbo lump crab*
- *¼ cup panko (Japanese style bread crumbs)*
- *1 pound baby spinach*
- *olive oil to sauté*
- *salt and pepper to taste*
- *Champagne Dijon Cream (recipe follows)*
- *Red Pepper Coulis (recipe follows)*

Preparation

IN A large stainless steel mixing bowl, whisk the egg, mustard, mayonnaise, lemon juice, Old Bay, Worcestershire, and chives together. Lightly toss the crabmeat in breadcrumbs and then in the dressing so that the crab is coated, but not broken into small pieces.

HEAT oven to 350 degrees. Form the crab mixture into 18 1-ounce balls and bake in the oven for 7 minutes. Wilt the spinach in olive oil with salt and pepper. To serve, ring the plate with 1½ ounces of Champagne Dijon Cream Sauce and place the wilted spinach in a pile in the center of the plate. Streak the plate with Roasted Red Pepper Coulis and place 3 crab cakes in a triangle on top of the sauce.

Serves 6

For the Champagne Dijon Cream Sauce

- *1 teaspoon shallot, finely diced*
- *½ teaspoon garlic, finely chopped*
- *clarified butter to sauté*
- *¼ cup champagne*
- *1 cup heavy cream*
- *1 tablespoon Dijon mustard*
- *salt and white pepper to taste*

SWEAT the shallots and garlic in a small amount of clarified butter. Deglaze with the champagne and reduce by half. Add the cream and scald. Add the Dijon and reduce to a nappe, thick enough to coat the back of a spoon. Season with salt and white pepper to taste.

For the Roasted Red Pepper Coulis

- *2 red bell peppers*

ROAST the red bell peppers on a hot grill until they are charred black. Place the peppers in a sealed container to steam for at least 15 minutes. Peel the skin from the peppers and remove stem and seeds. In a drink blender, blend until smooth and put into a squirt bottle.

Grilled Ruby Red Trout

with Rosemary Pine Nut Risotto and Charred Tomato Beurre Blanc

Ingredients

6 8- to 10-ounce ruby red trout filets
Rosemary Pine Nut Risotto (recipe follows)
Charred Tomato Beurre Blanc (recipe follows)
Roasted Red Pepper Coulis (see recipe under Crab Cakes)
leek greens, thinly sliced, to garnish

Preparations

GRILL the trout filets until done. To serve, spoon the Rosemary Pine Nut Risotto in a strip in the center of the plate, and ladle the Charred Tomato Beurre Blanc on the left side of the risotto. Place a grilled trout filet on the risotto, leaning to the left. Streak in a zigzag fashion with Roasted Red Pepper Coulis, and top with the leek greens. Serve with your choice of vegetables on the right side of the plate.

Serves 6

For the Rosemary Pine Nut Risotto

¼ cup pine nuts
1 ounce clarified butter
1 small red onion, finely diced
1 tablespoon garlic, chopped
2 cups Arborio rice
½ cup white wine
1 pinch saffron
1½ tablespoons rosemary, chopped
6 cups chicken stock
2 ounces chilled butter
2 tablespoons chives, chopped
salt and pepper to taste

IN A large saucepot, toast the pine nuts in clarified butter until lightly browned. Add the red onion and garlic, and sweat until tender. Add the Arborio rice, stir to coat in butter, then add the white wine and burn off the alcohol. Add the saffron, rosemary, and stock. Bring to a boil, reduce to simmer, and cook for 20 minutes, stirring often. Finish with the chilled butter and chives, and season to taste.

For the Charred Tomato Beurre Blanc

5 roma tomatoes, char grilled
2 cups white wine
2-3 shallots, chopped, roughly
7-8 sprigs of thyme
1 cup heavy cream
1 pound butter, cubed and chilled
salt and pepper to taste

IN A stainless steel saucepot add the tomatoes, white wine, shallots, and thyme. Reduce the wine by half, add cream and reduce by half again. On a low flame, whisk in the butter a few pieces at a time, while mashing the tomatoes. Season to taste and strain.

Roasted Beef Tenderloin

with Seared Foie Gras, Fried Onion Rings, and Port Reduction

Ingredients

- 4 *pounds Yukon Gold potatoes, peeled*
- ¾ *cup garlic cloves*
- *olive oil to sauté*
- ½ *pound butter*
- 1 *pint heavy cream*
- *salt and white pepper to taste*
- 3 *pounds beef tenderloin*
- 6 *slices foie gras*
- *Fried Onion Rings (recipe follows)*
- *Port Reduction (recipe follows)*
- *Fresh thyme and rosemary sprigs, for garnish*

Preparation

BOIL the potatoes until tender. In a sauté pan, cover the garlic in oil and cook on low until the garlic is tender, then strain. Purée the garlic. Melt the butter in the cream. Mash the potatoes with the garlic purée, add the butter and cream mixture and mash again. Season to taste, and keep warm for serving.

HEAT the oven to 350 degrees. Season the beef with salt and pepper. Sear the outside of the beef on a grill and roast in the oven until desired temperature is reached. In a smoking hot pan, very quickly sear the foie gras.

TO SERVE, place the mashed potatoes in the center of the plate and top with two 4-ounce slices of tenderloin. Ladle 2 ounces of the Port Reduction over the meat and lay the foie gras on top of the beef. Place the Fried Onion Rings on top and serve with your choice of vegetables. Garnish with sprigs of thyme and rosemary tops.

Serves 6

For the Onion Rings

- 1 *small red onion, sliced thin and soaked in buttermilk*
- 1 *cup flour*
- 1 *pinch cayenne pepper*
- ½ *teaspoon garlic powder*
- ½ *teaspoon white pepper*
- ½ *teaspoon salt*
- *oil for frying*

MIX the flour, cayenne pepper, garlic, powder, white pepper, and salt. Coat the rings in the flour mix and fry until golden brown.

For the Port Reduction Sauce

- 1 *cup port*
- 1-2 *shallots, rough chopped*
- 3-4 *sprigs thyme*
- 1 *cup demi-glace*
- 1 *ounce chilled butter*
- *salt and pepper to taste*

BURN the alcohol from the port. Add the shallot, thyme, and demi-glace. Bring to a boil, reduce to a simmer, and reduce the liquid to 1½ cups. Add the butter and season to taste, then strain and reserve for serving.

Main Street in Telluride circa 1885, showing L.G. Denison's grocery store, S.R. Fitzgarrald's law office, Tryan's hardware store, Charles Oderfeld's general merchandise, Telluride House Lodging and Bath House, and W.H. Stewart's hardware store.

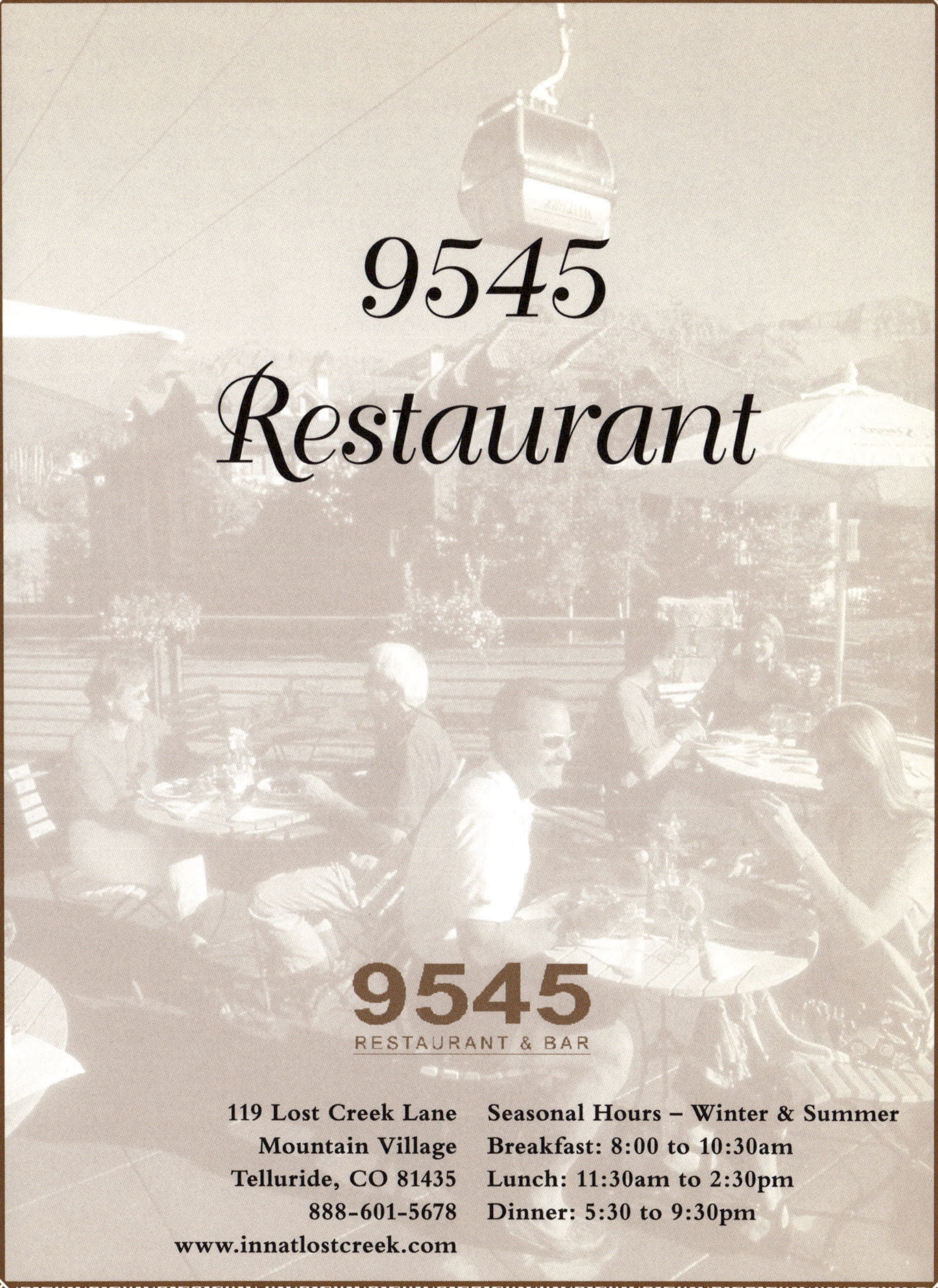
9545
Restaurant
9545
RESTAURANT & BAR
119 Lost Creek Lane
Mountain Village
Telluride, CO 81435
888-601-5678
www.innatlostcreek.com
Seasonal Hours – Winter & Summer
Breakfast: 8:00 to 10:30am
Lunch: 11:30am to 2:30pm
Dinner: 5:30 to 9:30pm

9545 Restaurant

Daniel Rosa, Executive Chef

The sumptuous accommodations at the Inn at Lost Creek provide the perfect spot for the 9545 Restaurant & Bar, named for the elevation at the Mountain Village. Although you can drive to the village, taking the spectacular gondola ride which whisks guests to and from the lovely town of Telluride is part of the fun.

Just a short walk from the terminal of the nation's only public gondola system, the restaurant offers special pampering for skiers in winter. They can check their skis with 9545's ski attendant and exchange their ski boots for a pair of the Inn's popular animal slippers before sitting down for a delectable lunch. In summer, the outdoor patio offers shaded dining under large umbrellas while you take in the stunning San Juan Mountains and the lively Mountain Village scene, including the sunset concerts. The interior offers intimate dining with heavy wood accents in modern designs of wood weaving sprinkled throughout the rooms. The tables are decked out with crisp linen napkins to accent the polished wood and the simplicity of the design.

Menus at 6545 Restaurant & Bar may change occasionally to ensure the freshest seasonal ingredients available from fine food suppliers. Ecologically sustainable fisheries provide "24 hour" fresh seafood, shipped directly to the restaurant. "Farm to kitchen" produce is primarily local and regional, and organic breads are baked locally. In September 2005, Executive Chef Daniel Rosa joined the 9545 team. On a brief Colorado vacation, he discovered Telluride and was captivated by its beauty and small town appeal. Born in Puerto Rico, Chef Daniel learned about the importance of fresh fruits, vegetables, and seafood from his mother's masterful cooking. Moving to New York at the age of 13, he soon became involved in the restaurant business and enrolled in New York Restaurant School. After graduation he spent many years in Arizona, serving in several venues and meeting such notables as Julia Childs and Jacques Pepin. He served a seven-year stint at the Ritz Carlton in Phoenix and later took a position at Wrights Restaurant in the historic Biltmore Resort and Spa. Gradually, his own cooking methods evolved from his exposure to a wealth of managing styles, cooking systems, and techniques. He also came to realize that "American cuisine was no longer the world's culinary step-child", a philosophy that is much in evidence at 9545 Restaurant.

Diver Sea Scallops

with Frizzled Spinach, Crispy Carrots, and Citrus Beurre Blanc

This simple dish depends on the quality of the scallops. Go to a local sea monger and ask for dry packed or fresh scallops.

Ingredients

16 large scallops
1 tablespoon oil
1 pound baby spinach
4 ounces rendered bacon lardoons
Citrus Beurre Blanc (recipe follows)
Crispy Carrots (recipe follows)

Preparation

TO COOK scallops, heat medium sized sauté pan with a little oil. Pan sear the scallop until golden brown. Use pan to frizzle spinach with bacon. Place spinach in middle of plate with scallops surrounding. Drizzle Citrus Beurre Blanc sauce on the scallops and accompany with Crispy Carrots.

Serves 4

For the Citrus Beurre Blanc

½ pound butter
2 tablespoons lime juice
1 cup white wine
1 tablespoon shallots
1 bay leaf
1 clove garlic coarse chopped

TO MAKE sauce, cut butter into 1 inch cubes and chill. Then combine lime juice, white wine, shallots, bay leaf, and garlic. Reduce by 80% and add one cube of butter at a time until sauce is formed. Strain and keep warm.

For the Crispy Carrots

2 large carrots
2 cups Canola oil for frying

SLICE carrots in a fine julienne on a mandolin or by hand to ⅛ inch thickness, as long as possible. Fry at 300 degrees for 3-5 minutes or until bubbles stop. Drain on paper towels and reserve at room temperature.

Sake Marinated, Apricot Kurobuta Pork Tenderloin

with Spicy Pear Ginger Chutney

This is our most popular menu item at 9545. The pork is truly sensational; Kurobuta pork is the highest quality because of its amazing flavor and breeding techniques. Other brands will work, although Kurobuta is preferred.

Ingredients

- *2 16-ounce Kurobuta pork tenderloins*
- *16 ounces sake, any type*
- *2 tablespoons ginger, minced*
- *2 cloves garlic, minced*
- *2 tablespoons shallots, minced*
- *1½ ounces canola oil*
- *Apricot Shallot Glaze (recipe follows)*
- *Ginger Pear Chutney (recipe follows)*

Preparation

CLEAN pork of all sinew, fat, and silver skin. To make marinade, combine sake, ginger, garlic, shallots, and oil with pork and refrigerate overnight.

HEAT oven to 350 degrees. Heat oil in pan and sear pork. Finish in oven until medium rare to medium temperature is reached. Let pork rest for 4 – 5 minutes, and then slice on bias.

HEAT oven to broil. Glaze pork with Apricot Shallot Glaze and place under broiler until sauce is bubbling.

TO SERVE, cut each tenderloin in halve and place on bed of Ginger Pear Chutney. This dish pairs well with wasabi mashed potatoes and grilled soy glazed baby bok choy.

Serves 4

For the Apricot Shallot Glaze

- *6 shallots, peeled and French cut*
- *1 tablespoon fresh ginger, minced*
- *1 clove garlic*
- *2 cups red wine vinegar*
- *8 ounces apricot preserves*
- *1 tablespoon soy sauce*
- *2 tablespoons cilantro, chopped*

COMBINE shallots, ginger, garlic, and vinegar. Reduce by 70%, add preserves and simmer for 8 minutes. Add soy sauce and cilantro. Let stand for 3 minutes and strain through fine chinois or tamp. Keep warm until use if not using right away.

For the Ginger Pear Chutney

2 lemons, halved
2 pears
1 cup rice wine vinegar
3 tablespoons ginger, minced, divided
1½ cups sugar

TO MAKE lemon water, place 1 quart of water in a large saucepan, squeeze the lemon halves into the water, and add the lemon halves. Peel and dice pears and place in lemon water. Sweat pears on low temperature to remove water. Strain and return to pan with vinegar and half the ginger. Reduce by half and add sugar. Let simmer for 15 minutes, add the rest of the ginger, and simmer for 15 minutes more. When thickened, remove from the pan and put in a stainless steel pan to shock it.

Haystack Mountain Goat Cheese Crusted Colorado Lamb Rack

with Port Wine and Paonia Cherry Reduction

Ingredients

- *2 racks lamb*
- *2 shallots, chopped*
- *2 cloves garlic, chopped*
- *½ cup vegetable oil*
- *1 sprig rosemary*
- *1 sprig thyme*
- *1½ teaspoons fresh cracked black peppercorns, divided*
- *2 tablespoons chives*
- *1 tablespoon thyme*
- *1 tablespoon rosemary*
- *1 pound Haystack Mountain goat cheese*
- *Port Wine and Paonia Cherry Reduction (recipe follows)*

Preparation

FULLY French the lamb racks, removing all sinew from the bones. Cut racks into 4-bone portions. Marinate overnight with the shallots, garlic, oil, rosemary sprig, thyme sprig, and ½ teaspoon of the cracked black peppercorns.

HEAT oven to 350 degrees. While preparing the herbs for the crust, bring the goat cheese up to room temperature. Finely chop the chives, leaf the thyme, and chop the rosemary. Add these and the remaining 1 teaspoon of cracked black peppercorns to the goat cheese. Mix well by hand, then reserve in a covered container in a cool area of the kitchen.

HEAT large sauté pan with vegetable oil until smoking hot. Season the lamb with salt and pepper, then sear the lamb, fat side down, until golden brown. Flip lamb and sear the other side. Finish in a 350-degree oven for 6-8 minutes for medium rare temperature, and remove from oven.

HEAT oven to broil. Let lamb rest for 4 minutes, then crust each rack with 4 ounces of the goat cheese mixture. Heat crust under the broiler until golden brown. Slice the lamb into 2-bone portions. Plate the lamb in a pool of the Port Wine Reduction. This dish pairs well with bacon wrapped asparagus and homemade mashed potatoes.

Serves 4

For the Port Wine and Paonia Cherry Reduction

1 bottle your favorite port
1 pound stoned Paonia cherries
1 teaspoon turbinado sugar
2 cloves garlic, chopped
2 shallots, chopped
1 sprig rosemary
1 sprig thyme
1 tablespoon fresh cracked pepper
salt to taste

PLACE the port, Paonia cherries and sugar into a saucepan with the garlic and the shallots. Reduce at a very low simmer (not boiling) until a syrupy consistency is achieved. Add the rosemary, thyme, and black pepper and steep for the last 10 minutes of the reduction. Strain through a chinois and reserve the sauce, discard all other ingredients.

Haystack Mountain Goat Cheese Crusted Colorado Lamb Rack

Croissant Bread Pudding and Apple Compote

Serve with your favorite ice cream. French Vanilla is what we prefer. This is wonderful on a cold winter night after a long day of snowboarding, or enjoying the beautiful San Juan Mountains.

Ingredients

8 stale croissants
10 egg yolks
6 whole eggs
1 cup sugar
32 ounces heavy cream
1 tablespoon vanilla
Apple Compote (recipe follows)

Preparation

HEAT oven to 300 degrees. Cut croissants into ½-inch dice and set aside. Combine eggs and sugar and whisk until frothy. Combine with cream and vanilla, strain; mix with croissants, and let sit. Bake at 300 degrees for 30 minutes. Serve with Apple Compote.

For the Apple Compote

2 apples
½ cup sugar
½ teaspoon cinnamon

CUT apples in ¼-inch dice and sauté in pan. When water begins to come out add sugar and cinnamon and mix. Let cook for 5 minutes. Serve on warm bread pudding.

Argentine Grille
at Rico Hotel

124 S. Glasgow Ave, Hwy 145
Rico, CO 81332
800-365-1971
www.ricohotel.com

Dinner Tuesday through Sunday
5:30pm – 9:00pm
Sunday Brunch 9:00am – 2:00pm

Argentine Grille at Rico Hotel

Eamon O'Hara, Chef

Rico, Colorado is nestled in the majestic San Juan Mountains of southwestern Colorado and offers a unique opportunity to view a mountain town as it may have appeared decades ago. In 1833 Antoine Robidoux and a group of trappers searched for beaver along the upper Dolores River. While there, they discovered evidence that Spanish prospectors had previously processed precious metals in the area. The trappers moved on when they didn't find any gold or silver but in the mid-1860s, prospectors returned to stake claims. With the land to the south controlled by Ute Indians, it was difficult to get supplies to the miners until the Rio Grande Southern Railroad arrived in Rico in 1891, connecting the town with Durango and Ridgway. By 1892 the Rico had a population of nearly 5,000 with twenty-three saloons and a three-block red light district. With the slump in the price of silver in 1893, the town rapidly started losing population. Today, there are only about 250 yearlong residents.

Today, the sleepy little town is being rediscovered and tourism is booming. Located on the San Juan Scenic Byway, Rico is just a thirty-minute drive from Telluride, and one and one half hours from Durango. The Rico Hotel was originally constructed in 1926 to serve as a boardinghouse for miners. It was turned into a hotel in the "boom" of the 1940s. The hotel has gone through several major remodels, and now serves as a charming bed and breakfast inn with a four-star restaurant, The Argentine Grille. Many of the reclaimed mining materials have been tastefully used in the remodels.

The Argentine Grille offers fine cuisine in a comfortable, rustic setting. The cozy yellow interior has a bar, an open kitchen, and rough-hewn wooden tables. The atmosphere is casual and relaxed. Chef Eamon O'Hara, originally from the west coast of Ireland, received his culinary training in the United Kingdom. After coming to the United States, he held the position of Executive Sous Chef at the prestigious Bel Air in Los Angeles, California, where he had the privilege of working with Wolfgang Puck. He also served as the Chef at the Peaks in Telluride. Chef O'Hara favors the use of local organic meats and produce, giving the grille a distinctively regional flavor. Signature dishes include such succulent offerings as Crispy Crab Cakes with Cilantro Cream and Moroccan Style Grilled Leg of Lamb.

Olathe Sweet Corn Bisque

with Cilantro Pesto

Olathe corn is a local Colorado corn available from the town of the same name from late August through September. Sambal olek, a Vietnamese chili paste, is available in most supermarkets in the Asian section. Raw pumpkin seeds should be available at the local supermarket as well.

Ingredients

- *3 cups Olathe sweet corn, cleaned and shucked*
- *2 quarts heavy whipping cream*
- *salt and white pepper to taste*
- *1 pinch cayenne pepper*
- *Cilantro Pesto (recipe follows)*

Preparation

IN A heavy bottomed 2-quart sauce pan over medium heat, bring the corn and cream to a boil, stirring constantly. Reduce heat and simmer for 30 minutes, carefully watching that the cream does not boil over, until the liquid is reduced by 1/3. Place the corn-cream mixture into a bar blender, only filling to half capacity. Place the lid on securely and press down with your hand so the lid will not move. Blend until the mixture is smooth. Repeat this process for the rest of the cream and corn. Strain through a medium metal sieve and keep hot until serving.

TO SERVE, warm 4 soup bowls. Ladle in the soup, garnish with a pinch of cayenne pepper and Cilantro Pesto. Serve immediately.

Serves 4

For the Cilantro Pesto

- *1 teaspoon cilantro, chopped*
- *¼ teaspoon Parmesan cheese, grated*
- *¼ teaspoon pumpkin seeds, lightly toasted and finely chopped*
- *½ teaspoon freshly squeezed limejuice*
- *⅛ teaspoon sambal olek*

COMBINE cilantro, Parmesan, pumpkin seeds, limejuice, and sambal olek. Use within 4 hours for ultimate freshness.

Masa-Crusted Crisp Crab Cakes

with Jicama-Apple Slaw and Cilantro Cream

Ingredients

- *1 pound blue crab claw meat (canned)*
- *1 tablespoon red bell pepper, finely chopped and sautéed*
- *1 medium clove garlic, finely chopped and sautéed*
- *1 tablespoon cilantro, finely chopped*
- *2 tablespoons mayonnaise*
- *1 teaspoon Dijon mustard*
- *1 medium lemon, juice from*
- *salt and pepper to taste*
- *½ cup masa harina*
- *¼ cup olive oil*
- *Jicama-Apple Slaw (recipe follows)*
- *Cilantro Cream (recipe follows)*

Preparation

COMBINE crabmeat, bell pepper, garlic, cilantro, mayonnaise, mustard, lemon juice, and salt and pepper in a non-reactive bowl. Refrigerate until needed.

DIVIDE the crab mix into 4 sections and shape into balls. Dust lightly in the masa harina. Heat a medium sized non-stick pan with the olive oil. Shape crab into large medallions and place in pan carefully. Cook for 2 minutes or until brown, then carefully turn over to brown the other side for another 2 minutes.

TO SERVE, place one crab cake on each plate with a small amount of Cilantro Cream and some Jicama-Apple Slaw. Serve immediately.

Serves 4

For the Jicama-Apple Slaw

- *1 medium sized gala apple, finely diced*
- *2 tablespoons jicama, peeled and finely diced*
- *1 teaspoon red onion, finely diced*
- *1 tablespoon red bell pepper, finely diced*
- *1 lime, juice from*
- *salt and pepper to taste*

COMBINE apple, jicama, onion, bell pepper and limejuice in a non-reactive bowl just before serving. Season with salt and pepper to taste.

For the Cilantro Cream

- *⅛ cup white wine (Chablis or chardonnay)*
- *1 quart heavy whipping cream*
- *¼ cup chicken or vegetable broth*
- *1 tablespoon Cilantro Pesto (see corn bisque recipe)*

IN A heavy bottomed saucepan over medium heat, bring the white wine to a boil and reduce it by half. Add the chicken or vegetable broth and cream and reduce liquid by half, being careful no to let it boil over. Combine pesto and one cup of the cream sauce just before serving.

Grilled "Gaucho Style" Beef Tenderloin
with Parsley Chimichurri

Ingredients

1 20-ounce beef filet
Parsley Chimichurri (recipe follows)

Preparation

MARINATE the beef in half the Parsley Chimichurri for at least 20 minutes. Grill to required doneness. Slice and serve with the rest of the sauce.

Serves 4

For the Parsley Chimichurri

- *½ bunch parsley, finely chopped*
- *4 cloves garlic, peeled and finely chopped*
- *1 tablespoon yellow onion, finely chopped*
- *1 teaspoon capers, finely chopped*
- *½ teaspoon Dijon mustard*
- *¼ cup red wine vinegar*
- *1 tablespoon extra virgin olive oil*
- *salt and pepper to taste*

COMBINE parsley, garlic, onion, capers, mustard, vinegar, and olive oil. Season with salt and pepper.

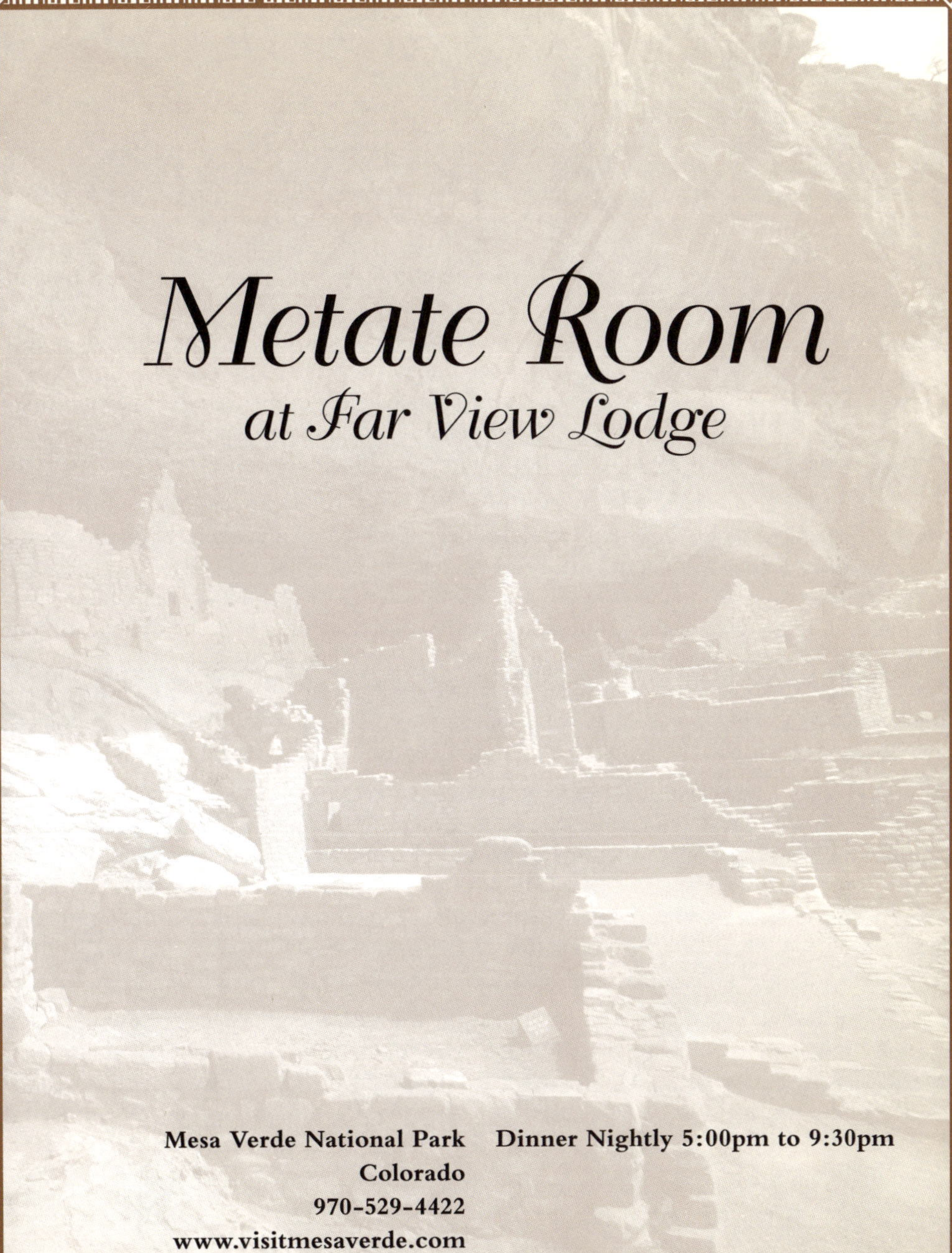

Metate Room

at Far View Lodge

Mesa Verde National Park
Colorado
970-529-4422
www.visitmesaverde.com

Dinner Nightly 5:00pm to 9:30pm

Metate Room at Far View Lodge

Todd Hanier, Executive Chef
Jeff Mobley, Sommelier

The Metate Room offers a feast for the eyes as well as the taste buds. Situated in the Far View Lodge in Mesa Verde National Park, this beautiful restaurant offers a good reason to stay inside the park when you come to explore the world-famous cliff dwellings of the Ancestral Puebloans. The rustic Far View Lodge offers 150 comfortable rooms, including dozens of newly renovated and upgraded kiva-style rooms. The rooms are spread out on a spectacular butte with views facing south across the park.

The restaurant displays fantastic views over the mesas and canyons through the south-facing over-sized windows, and the two-level design allows all guests to enjoy the magnificent view. The adobe style room features a dark-beamed wood ceiling with mission-style furniture with Native American artwork and place settings. The Ancestral Puebloans raised corn, beans, and squash, gathered nuts and herbs, and hunted wild game. Celebrating their culture, the menus at the Metate Room are based on these staples, with a few modern favorites also included. Look for such favorites as quail, buffalo, and elk on the menu, as well as many standard favorites dressed up with southwestern spices. The wine list is classified by style of wine, not varietal, helping the lay person choose the best pairing for their entrée.

Aramark Parks & Resorts, which operates Mesa Verde National Park, is committed to the Sustainable Cuisine movement, offering foods grown and harvested in ways that are most healthful and least harmful to the environment. For example, the Metate Room only serves seafood from species populations that are not currently under threat of extinction by over fishing. It also uses organic produce whenever possible, and supports the local agricultural communities, from Shade Tree grown coffee and Hearst grass-fed beef.

A Colorado native, Executive Chef Todd Halnier started his culinary career as Executive Sous Chef for Denver's Wilshire Inn. Later, he spent three years as Executive Chef for Josef's Restaurant in Gunnison. A graduate of Denver's School of Culinary Arts, Chef Halnier came to Mesa Verde in December 2002, and assumed the position of Executive Chef the next year. His commitment to using organic and eco-friendly ingredients and locally grown, sustainable products whenever possible has helped lift the quality of the Metate Room's cuisine to an even higher level.

Colorado Corn and Crab Cake

Ingredients

- 3 *ears Colorado sweet corn (Olathe or Ute Mountain)*
- 2 *pounds lump crabmeat*
- 2 *ounces heavy mayonnaise*
- 1 *egg*
- *salt and pepper to taste*
- ½ *teaspoon Old Bay Seasoning*
- *Japanese bread crumbs as needed*
- *Oil to fry*
- 4 *ounces micro greens*
- *Thai sweet chili sauce*

Preparation

ROAST the corn in its husks on a grill until very dark. Peel the husk and scrape kernels off the cob. Pick crab to remove any shells and squeeze out the juice. Add the corn, mayonnaise, egg, salt and pepper, and Old Bay. Lightly mix to combine, but keep crabmeat as whole as possible. Shape into 6-ounce balls and roll in bread crumbs, packing balls to coat completely. Place in a pan, and press to flatten. Pan fry in oil until golden. Serve with micro greens and Thai chili sauce.

Serves 6

Wine suggestion: Sutcliff Chardonnay 2004

Roasted Garlic-Eggplant and Brie Soup

Ingredients

- 4 eggplants
- 1 cup olive oil, divided
- 20 cloves garlic
- 2 yellow onions
- ¾ gallon of stock, chicken or vegetable
- salt and pepper to taste
- 1 pound Brie cheese
- 2 cups heavy cream
- roux or cornstarch as needed
- ½ cup toasted pine nuts

Preparation

HEAT oven to 350 degrees. Cut eggplant in half lengthwise. Score the flesh side, rub with ½ cup of the oil, and roast until brown, approximately 35-45 minutes. Simultaneously pan roast the garlic in the remaining ½ cup oil for 10-15 minutes until brown.

ROUGH chop the onion and sauté in a large soup pot until soft. Add the stock, roasted eggplant and garlic. Bring to a boil; add salt and pepper to taste and the Brie cheese. Continue to boil for a few minutes. Remove from heat and purée with a hand mixer or blender. Strain liquid into another pot and add the heavy cream. Discard leftover pulp. Bring soup back to a boil and thicken with roux or slurry to heavy, creamy consistency. Garnish with toasted pine nuts.

Serves 8

Wine suggestion: Stag's Leap Viognier 2004

Hickory Smoked Buffalo Ribeye

with Gorgonzola Sauce

Ingredients

- *1 pound hickory wood chips*
- *3 pounds buffalo rib roast, boneless*
- *cracked black pepper, to taste*
- *Gorgonzola Sauce (recipe follows)*

Preparation

ON A hot outdoor grill, add the wood chips and let them begin to smoke. Rub the rib with pepper, place in the smoky grill and cover. Let smoke for 10 minutes, or until brown from the smoke. Let rib rest in refrigerator for 10 minutes. Cut into four 12-ounce steaks. Reserve in refrigerator. To serve, finish steaks on the grill to desired temperature. Serve with your favorite starch and the Gorgonzola Sauce over the top.

Serves 4

Wine suggestion: Chateau St. Jean 'Cinq', Sonoma

For the Gorgonzola Sauce

- *4 shallots*
- *2 tablespoons olive oil, divided*
- *1 cup heavy cream*
- *4 ounces Gorgonzola cheese*
- *1 cup spinach leaves*
- *salt and pepper to taste*

HEAT oven to 350 degrees. Roast the shallots in 1 tablespoon of the olive oil until brown, approximately 10-15 minutes. Peel and discard the outer layers of shallots. Rough chop the inner layers. Sauté in a saucepot for 1-2 minutes with the remaining olive oil. Add heavy cream and reduce by ¼. Add cheese and continue to cook for about 5 minutes. Add the spinach and remove from heat. Adjust seasoning with salt and pepper. Serve warm.

A group of tourists posing in the reconstructed Cliff Palace ruins circa 1920.

East by Southwest
Durango Colorado
EAST by Southwest
Sushi • Steak • Fusion
160 E College Drive
Durango, CO 81301
970-247-5533
www.eastbysouthwest.com
Lunch:
Monday – Saturday 11:30am – 3:00pm
Dinner:
Nightly, starting at 5:00pm
Happy Hour: 5:00 to 6:30pm

East by Southwest

Sergio Verduzco, Chef/Owner
Hydi Verduzco, Owner

East by Southwest adds a delightful change of atmosphere to the historic Old West town of Durango. Located on the corner of East 2nd Avenue and College Drive, the restaurant has been serving Pan Asian cuisine since 2002. The sleek interior invites guests to relax at individual tables or at the sushi bar, where you can gaze on the spotless cases of fresh sushi grade fish. There is also a Tatami Room, where guests are seated on the floor, on tatami mats, and dine in the traditional Japanese style. This room has become quite popular for small groups, as it seats about twenty, and can be separated from the main dining room.

A native of Mexico, Chef Sergio Verduzco is a graduate of the Culinary Institute of America. He and his wife and partner, Hydi, are both graduates of the College of Hotel and Restaurant Administration at the University of Nevada, Las Vegas. With over two decades of culinary experience, Chef Sergio was the Executive Chef at the Bel Air Hotel Costa Careyes in Mexico and then served as Chef de Cuisine for the Peaks Hotel and Spa in Telluride. In 1999, Chef Sergio enrolled in the California Sushi Academy, furthering his culinary education.

The restaurant's cuisine features Japanese and Pacific Rim fare, with interesting Latino and southwestern accents added to many of the dishes. For those who have not yet grown accustomed to sushi, the restaurant also serves many cooked dishes. The Verduzcos feature hormone-free beef, and chicken, and use many organic products, in order to create cuisine that is low fat, light, and healthy. There are extensive options for vegetarians, as well as many stir-fry dishes and noodles. The seafood is obtained from a special seafood broker who supplies some of the best seafood available in the world.

Unique beverages are available at East by Southwest, both alcoholic and non-alcoholic. A full bar is offered, as well as an extensive selection of sake, Asian beers, and wines. Several different herbal tea blends are offered and are well described on the beverage menu. All teas and herbal extracts are custom blended for the restaurant by Hummingbird Herbals. There is also a menu of tonics, aphrodisiacs, and elixirs, all mixed with Tahitian noni juice, and described in detail for the adventurous.

East by Southwest appeals to the devoted sushi aficionado as well as to anyone who enjoys the unique flavors of Asian foods. The wait staff is knowledgeable about the offerings, and is always ready to help guests with selections, making this a great place to introduce newcomers to the delights of Asian cuisine.

Kobe Beef-wrapped Asparagus

with Yuzu and Truffle Oil

This simple dish is a layered kaleidoscope of flavor and texture. The first thing to stimulate the senses is the hedonistic scent of the truffles, followed by the perfumed taste of the yuzu citrus. The charred marbling of the Kobe beef brings a full steak flavor, followed finally by the crisp bite of the fresh asparagus. The yuzu citrus juice is available on the Internet or in Japanese food markets. You can also substitute a blend of equal parts of mandarin orange and lemon juice.

Ingredients

16 spears fresh pencil asparagus
16 ounces Kobe beef sirloin (or Prime Black Angus sirloin)
Hawaiian pink salt, Fleur de Sel, or sea salt (any will do)
1 ounce low sodium soy sauce
1 ounce yuzu citrus juice
1 ounce black truffle oil

Preparation

CUT the woody ends off the asparagus, and peel, blanch, and chill. Cut the beef into 4-ounce steaks. Thinly slice each steak across the grain into 5 slices. Shingle the sliced beef in between two sheets of plastic wrap. Pound the meat with a mallet to make a sheet about 8 by 4 inches in size. Carefully remove the top plastic layer. Place 4 prepared asparagus in pairs end to end in the middle of the beef sheet. Sprinkle with salt. Using the remaining plastic sheet, roll the asparagus like a sushi roll inside the meat with the crown ends sticking out at both ends. Remove the remaining plastic sheet. If you have a rolling matt, press and shape the beef roll tightly. Place the roll on a metal sheet pan, and sear the outside perimeter of the roll with a brûlée or propane torch. Slice into 8 symmetrical pieces. Arrange the slices decoratively on a plate with the asparagus ends sticking up. Pour ½ ounce of soy sauce and 1 teaspoon of yuzu juice over the top, enough to create a shallow pool. Finish with a drizzle of truffle oil. Enjoy!

Serves 4

Mahi Mahi "Dorado" Ceviche

This dish takes me back to the beaches of Jalisco, Mexico where I worked as Executive Chef of The Bel Air Hotel & Spa in Costa Careyes. It is very popular for happy hour at East by Southwest and it brings a Latino touch to our offerings. This basic ceviche recipe also works well with any non-oily fish or seafood. Note: regular limes will also work for this recipe, however key limes have more flavor and acidity.

Ingredients

1 pound fresh mahi mahi filet
15 key limes, cut in half & divided
Pico de Gallo (recipe follows)
1 teaspoon kosher or sea salt
corn tortilla chips or tostadas to accompany
fresh cilantro sprigs for garnish
lime wedges for garnish

Preparation

DICE the fish into ½-inch cubes. In a non-reactive bowl, marinate the fish in the salt and the juice of 10 of the key limes for at least one hour, under refrigeration. The acid in the limejuice will actually cook the fish. It should change from translucent to white in color. Drain the fish in a colander and rinse slightly to remove any fishiness.

TOSS the marinated fish with the Pico de Gallo and the juice from the remaining 5 limes and season with kosher salt to taste. I also like to add a dash of Tabasco sauce to round out the flavors. Be careful, as it will also add more heat.

SERVE the ceviche in a bowl surrounded by corn tortilla chips, or it can be served with tostadas. Garnish with fresh cilantro sprigs and serve with extra lime wedges on the side.

Serves 10

For the Pico de Gallo

5 ripe roma tomatoes, de-seeded and cut into ¼-inch cubes
½ yellow onion, small dice
1 bunch fresh cilantro
5 fresh jalapenos, de-seeded and diced

IN A non-reactive bowl, mix the tomatoes, onion, cilantro, and jalapenos. For a spicier version of the Pico de Gallo I prefer to use fresh Habanero chiles. If using Habaneros, cut the amount of chilies in half. Take care to use rubber or latex gloves when working with chiles to avoid burning your fingertips.

Chilean Sea Bass "Miso Yaki"

This dish is a top seller in our restaurant. "Miso yaki" means broiled with miso in Japanese, and this sweet miso marinade works well with any oily fish. When broiled it creates a deliciously delicate glaze. It also works as a preservative while tenderizing the fish. Black cod is wonderful broiled in this manner.

Ingredients

- 2 *cups white miso paste*
- 2 *cups sweet mirin cooking wine*
- 1 *cup seasoned rice vinegar*
- ¾ *cup granulated sugar*
- 3 *pounds Chilean sea bass*
- 1½ *pounds fresh asparagus spears, slightly steamed*
- 8 *cups steamed white rice*
- *pickled ginger and slivered scallions to garnish*

Preparation

HEAT the oven to broil at high heat. In a non-reactive bowl, mix the miso paste, mirin, vinegar, and sugar using an electric wand mixer. Cut the fish into 6-ounce portions, cutting on a bias, about 2 inches thick. Marinate the fish overnight, covered and under refrigeration. This is very important as the marinade needs this time to work its magic. Spread the fish in a single layer on a ceramic baking dish without overcrowding the fish. Lower the heat slightly and broil the fish until a blistered glaze forms and the fish flakes apart when pressed with a fork. Take care not to burn the top of the fish before it has a chance to cook thoroughly.

TO SERVE, place the fish over a bed of steamed asparagus spears with a side of steamed sticky rice. Garnish with pickled ginger and slivered scallions. Cucumber Sunomono Salad is also a great side dish for this fish. See recipe under Beef Teriyaki Skewers.

Serves 8

Kurobuta Pork Chop Adobo

with Apple & Jalapeno Chutney, Black Bean Sauce, and Garlic Mashed Potatoes

At East by Southwest we serve all organic meats, and Kurobuta Japanese Black Hog is the premier organic pork. The marbling is similar to Kobe beef, producing superb tender meat. You can also use regular pork, but make sure to cook it above 150 degrees to avoid pathogens. This dish is a prime example of our fusion style, combining a Japanese delicacy with the flavors of my Latino roots.

Ingredients

- 8 *dry Guajillo chilies or red New Mexico chilies*
- 10 *cloves garlic*
- ½ *yellow onion*
- 1 *cup sugar*
- 10 *ounces orange juice*
- 1 *cup apple cider vinegar*
- 2 *tablespoons salt*
- 5 *roma tomatoes, rough chopped*
- 1 *teaspoon fresh thyme leaves*
- 1 *ounce Achiote (annatto seed paste, available in Latino food markets)*
- 1 *Kurobuta Pork Rib Rack, 3-4 pounds*
- 1 *sprig fresh thyme or rosemary, to garnish*
- *Black Bean Sauce (recipe follows)*
- *Roasted Garlic Yukon Gold Mashed Potatoes (recipe follows)*
- *Apple & Jalapeno Chutney (recipe follows)*
- *fresh thyme, rosemary, or chopped parsley for garnish*

Preparation

REMOVE seeds and stems from the dry chilies. Place the chilies on a sheet pan and toast slightly in a hot oven until they release their aroma. Be careful not to scorch them. Soak the chilies in hot water for 30 minutes. Discard most of the soaking liquid, leaving enough to purée the chilies in a blender. Purée the chilies, then add the garlic, onion, sugar, orange juice, vinegar, salt, tomatoes, thyme, and Achiote, making sure all is blended well. Cut the pork rack into single bone chops. French the bones (scrape clean) and marinate in the adobo marinade overnight.

GRILL the marinated pork chops to medium rare. Kurobuta pork is pathogen free, so it can be served at this temperature. If you prefer, you may cook it to medium, but never well done. It is highly marbled and can dry out. Crisscross the grill marks on the pork chops for a nice visual appearance.

TO SERVE, ladle a pool of Black Bean Sauce onto a nice extended bowl or plate. Mound 3 ounces of the Garlic Mashed Potatoes over that, and prop up two pork chops on the potatoes with their bones crisscrossed. Top off the pork chops with the Apple & Jalapeno Chutney, and garnish with a sprig of fresh thyme or rosemary. You can also sprinkle the rim of the plate with chopped fresh parsley if you like.

Serves 6–7

For the Black Bean Sauce

- 3 *cups black turtle beans*
- 10 *cups water*
- ¼ *pound smoked bacon*
- ½ *onion, diced*
- 5 *cloves garlic, chopped*
- ¼ *teaspoon whole cumin, toasted and then ground in a spice or coffee grinder*
- *salt and pepper to taste*

SOAK the beans in additional water overnight before cooking. Cook the beans with the 10 cups water in a tightly covered pot until very tender, approximately 1 hour. Check periodically that the water doesn't evaporate completely; you may have to add more water.

RENDER the bacon, then add the onion and garlic and caramelize them well, without burning. Add this mix and the cumin to the beans, adding more water if needed. Simmer for 20 minutes. Remove from the heat and purée with a hand-held wand blender. The consistency should be like black bean soup: saucy and able to coat the back of a spoon. Adjust the seasoning to taste with salt and pepper. (To serve this as a black bean soup, just garnish it with sour cream, scallions, queso fresco crumbles, and cilantro.)

For the Roasted Garlic Yukon Gold Mashed Potatoes

- 3 *pounds Yukon Gold potatoes*
- 2 *cups heavy whipping cream*
- ¼ *pound whole butter*
- 1 *teaspoon fresh grated nutmeg*
- 10 *cloves garlic, roasted or sautéed golden*
- *salt and white pepper to taste*

PEEL the potatoes, cover with water and cook until fork tender, then drain in a colander. Bring the cream, butter, and nutmeg to a boil, remove from the fire, and keep warm. Pass the potatoes and garlic cloves through a food mill or potato press. If you don't have either one, mash the potatoes with a large fork and chop the garlic with a knife. Whip the potato and garlic mixture, and add the hot cream slowly. Be sure not to add too much, as it will make the mashed potatoes too thin. Adjust the seasoning to taste with salt and white pepper. A little white pepper goes a long way. Reserve for serving.

For the Apple & Jalapeno Chutney

- 4 *cups granulated sugar*
- 1 *cup water*
- ½ *cup unseasoned rice vinegar*
- 6 *Granny Smith apples, cored and diced in ¼-inch cubes, skin on*
- 1 *tablespoon dry red chili pepper flakes*
- 1 *yellow pimento, de-seeded and diced in very small cubes*
- 6 *fresh red jalapenos, de-seeded and diced in very small cubes*

IF GREEN jalapenos are used instead of red, add them to the chutney after it is cooked, during the cool down phase, to retain the green color of the jalapeno chilies. In a thick-bottomed stainless steel pot, dampen the sugar with the water and cook with a medium flame until it turns golden in color. Do not stir the sugar or it will re-crystallize. Add the vinegar to make a gastrique and allow to simmer for 5 minutes. Add the apples, chili flakes, pimento, and jalapenos. Cook at low heat for 30-40 minutes, stirring occasionally. Take care not to scorch it. Remove from the fire when it gets a candied look. Pour into a stainless steel bowl and cool down immediately over an ice bath. Reserve for serving.

Beef Teriyaki Skewers "Yakitori"

with Cucumber Sunomono Salad

Ingredients

- 1 2-pound flank steak
- 8-inch bamboo skewers
- ½ cup fresh ginger root, minced
- 1 tablespoon fresh garlic, minced
- 2 cups honey or brown sugar
- 1 pint mirin, sweet cooking wine
- 1 cup low sodium soy sauce
- ½ cup green scallions, minced
- ½ cup unseasoned rice vinegar
- Cucumber Sunomono Salad (recipe follows)
- toasted sesame seeds and slivered scallions to garnish

Preparation

CUT the flank steak into thin strips on an angle against the grain of the flesh. Thread the bamboo skewers lengthwise through the beef strips, at least 3 times so that the beef doesn't fall off the skewer while grilling. Combine the ginger, garlic, brown sugar, mirin, soy sauce, scallions, and rice vinegar. Marinate the skewers in this mixture overnight or for at least 4 hours, covered in refrigeration. Grill the skewers, preferably over charcoal, until done. Serve over a mound of Cucumber Sunomono Salad and garnish with toasted sesame seeds and slivered scallions.

Serves 6–7

For the Cucumber Sunomono Salad

- ½ cup sugar
- 1 cup seasoned rice vinegar (if unseasoned, add another ½ cup granulated sugar)
- ¼ cup low sodium soy sauce
- 1 teaspoon hon dashi bonito powder (available in the Asian food section of the supermarket)
- ¼ cup hot water
- 4 hot house or English cucumbers, skin on
- ¼ cup dehydrated wakame seaweed (optional, also in the Asian food section)
- ¼ cup toasted sesame seeds

DISSOLVE hon dashi powder in the hot water and combine it with the sugar, vinegar, and soy sauce. Wash the cucumbers well, cut in half lengthwise and slice crosswise as thin as possible. I recommend an Asian mandolin to get the best results. Regular cucumbers may be used, but they must be peeled, cut lengthwise in half, and the seeds scraped out with a spoon. Re-hydrate the seaweed. Soak the sliced cucumbers in salted water for 5 minutes and drain. Combine the seaweed, cucumbers, and dressing in a non-reactive bowl. Sprinkle with toasted sesame seeds before serving.

Berries & Choya with Ginger Ice Cream

This simple dessert is always a hit, and it is quick and easy to prepare. It can be served with your favorite ice cream. I recommend a high quality ice cream for the best impact.

Ingredients

- *1 pint ripe blackberries*
- *1 pint ripe raspberries*
- *1 pint ripe blueberries*
- *1 pint ripe strawberries, de-stemmed, and sliced*
- *8 ounces Choya plum wine*
- *¼ cup granulated sugar*
- *wonton skins (2 inch squares)*
- *canola oil to fry*
- *1 quart "Maeda En" Ginger Ice Cream*
- *powdered sugar for garnish*
- *fresh mint leaves for garnish*

Preparation

IN A non-reactive bowl, toss the berries with the granulated sugar and the plum wine. Allow the berries to macerate at least 1 hour. Cut the wonton skin squares by half into triangle shapes, and fry them in hot canola oil until crisp. Put the fried wonton skins over paper towels to absorb excess grease, and reserve them.

I LIKE to present this dessert in a large martini glass as follows. Place a large scoop of ice cream in the bottom of the glass. Top the ice cream with the macerated berries. Arrange the fried wonton triangles around the rim of the glass in a whirlwind pattern. Using a shaker filled with powdered sugar, sprinkle the wonton skins with the sugar and garnish the top of the berries with a sprig of fresh mint.

Serves 12

View over Durango circa 1880.

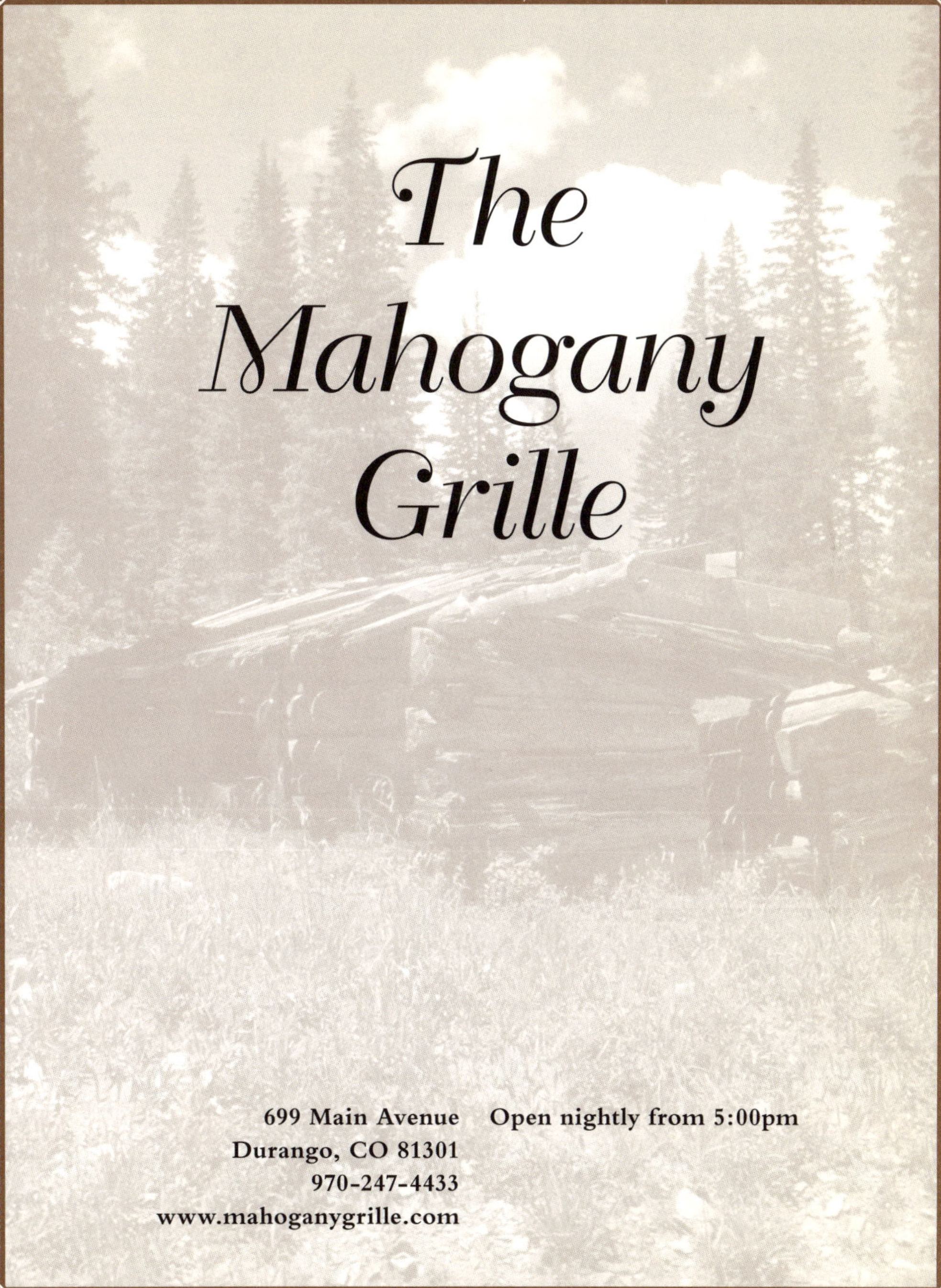

The Mahogany Grille

699 Main Avenue
Durango, CO 81301
970-247-4433
www.mahoganygrille.com

Open nightly from 5:00pm

The Mahogany Grille

Dave Cuntz, Executive Chef
Robert Muir, Executive Sous Chef

Established in 2004, The Mahogany Grille is an exquisite yet casual dining experience, combining sophisticated cuisine and a luxurious mahogany theme, with cool jazz and nightly entertainment. The Grille is located in the historic Strater Hotel in the heart of Durango. Henry Strater built the first of three sections of the building in 1887 for the main purpose of housing his pharmacy. He leased the space to Harry Rice, but forgot to exclude the space he wanted for his pharmacy. Harry demanded a premium for the space, prompting Henry to build the Columbia Hotel next door, hoping to put Harry out of business. Around 1900, Charles Stilwell purchased both buildings, joining them under the name of The Strater Hotel. The Barker family along with other members of the New Strater Corporation purchased the property in 1926. The last section of the building was added in 1938 and in 1953 the Barker family purchased the remaining stock.

The 2004 remodel of the area that houses The Mahogany Grille brought an exciting décor to the room, giving it a casual elegance that is in a style of its very own. The restaurant describes its cuisine as New American with international influences. Executive Chef Dave Cuntz came on board in September 2005. Raised in Denver, he arrived in Durango to attend Fort Lewis College where he received a BFA degree. During these early years, he also worked at the Chart House in Golden, took a tour abroad in Chambrey, France as an exchange student at the University of Savoi where he increased his knowledge of French cooking and traditions. Shortly after his graduation from college, he completed the Associates Degree Program at the New England Culinary Institute, followed by internships at the Flagstaff House in Boulder, and then at Equus Restaurant in Lousivlle, Kentucky. Over the next twelve years, he rose through the ranks at Equus to become the Executive Chef.

Executive Sous Chef, Robert Muir, started his culinary career by serving as Lead Cook and Apprentice at the Marriott Solana in Texas, and then moved to the Omni Mandalay Hotel at Los Colinas as the Chef's Apprentice and Garde Manger Supervisor. During this time he received many medals for his food creations at the Dallas food shows. Relocating to Durango in 2000, Robert worked at the Sheraton Tamarron Resort where he earned Chef certifications through the American Culinary Federation.

Fennel and Grapefruit Salad

with Tarragon Dijon Dressing

Ingredients

- *1 head fresh fennel, shaved thin*
- *16-20 segments ruby grapefruit*
- *8 slices prosciutto ham, sliced paper thin*
- *4 cups mixed baby greens*
- *1 cup Tarragon Dijon Dressing (recipe follows)*

Preparation

CHILL 4 salad plates. Place 1 cup of the greens on each plate and top with 3 pieces of shaved fennel. Place 2 slices of prosciutto ham, torn into shreds, on each plate. Then place 4-5 grapefruit segments around the salad. Finish with 1-2 ounces of Tarragon Dijon Dressing and enjoy!

Serves 4

For the Tarragon Dijon Dressing

- *½ cup white vinegar*
- *½ cup tarragon vinegar*
- *1½ tablespoons dried tarragon*
- *2 tablespoons parsley, chopped*
- *3 ounces smooth Dijon mustard*
- *1 dash balsamic vinegar*
- *4 cups olive oil blend*
- *salt & pepper to taste*

WHISK together all ingredients except olive oil. Then whisk in the oil and adjust seasoning with salt and pepper.

Yield: 2 quarts

Southwestern Salmon Tamales

with Fresh Tomato Gazpacho Sauce

Ingredients

- *1 package corn husks*
- *1 stick butter, melted*
- *4 pieces salmon filet, 5-6 ounces each*
- *salt and pepper to taste*
- *1 Anaheim chili, sliced into rings*
- *½ cup toasted pine nuts, roughly chopped*
- *1 bunch cilantro, roughly chopped*
- *Fresh Tomato Gazpacho Sauce*
- *whole toasted pine nuts for garnish*

Preparation

HEAT oven to 375 degrees. Soak corn husks in warm water overnight, or for at least 1 hour. Separate the corn husks into 8 individual pieces (the longer the better). Place 2 of the pieces together to form a canoe shaped piece. Brush butter on the inside of the husks. Place the salmon inside the corn husk. Brush the salmon with butter, and sprinkle with salt and pepper. Place 4 slices of Anaheim chilies across the top of the salmon and sprinkle with the pine nuts and cilantro. Encase with the corn husks, then cut a husk into strips and tie the encased salmon closed at each end and in the center. Place on a sheet pan and bake in the oven for 12 to 17 minutes. To serve, remove the center tie and 1 end tie. Remove the first husk and pull back the center section of the other husk to reveal the salmon. Ladle with the Fresh Tomato Gazpacho Sauce and a pinch of whole toasted pine nuts.

Serves 4

For the Fresh Tomato Gazpacho Sauce

- *½ small red onion, diced*
- *1 tablespoon fresh garlic, chopped*
- *½ stalk celery, diced small*
- *½ Anaheim chili, diced small*
- *2 large tomatoes, peeled, seeded, and diced*
- *1 splash white wine*
- *½ cup vegetable stock*
- *¼ bunch cilantro, chopped*
- *5 dashes Tabasco sauce*
- *salt and pepper to taste*
- *cornstarch*

SAUTÉ the onion, garlic, celery, and chilies for 3 – 5 minutes. Add the tomatoes and sauté for 2 more minutes. Deglaze with white wine, and then add the vegetable stock, cilantro, and Tabasco. Bring to a boil. Thicken with just a bit of cornstarch, being careful not to over thicken the mixture. Season to taste, serve warm.

Harvest Beef Tender Stew

Ingredients

- 2 *pounds beef tenderloin, cut into 1-inch cubes*
- 1 *quart red wine, divided*
- 1½ *tablespoons fresh rosemary, chopped*
- 1½ *tablespoons fresh sage, chopped*
- 2 *tablespoons fresh garlic, chopped*
- 1 *yellow onion, diced large*
- 2 *cups butternut squash, cut into large cubes*
- 2 *cups peeled potatoes, cut into large cubes*
- 5 *cups rich beef stock*
- *butter & flour to make a roux*
- *salt and pepper to taste*

Preparation

SAUTÉ beef until browned. The beef needs to be browned in a single layer in order to improve the browning. Deglaze with half of the red wine. Let the wine reduce by half, and then add the rosemary, sage, and garlic, and the rest of the wine. Add the onion, squash, potatoes, and beef stock, and cook until the meat is tender and flavorful. Adjust the seasonings with salt and pepper and thicken with a roux. Serve with seasoned puff pastry strips, sautéed green beans, and roasted tomatoes. Enjoy.

Serves 6 – 8

Broiled Duck Breast

with Honey Lavender Sauce and Goat Cheese Cakes

Ingredients

- *4 duck breasts with skin on, about 8 ounces each*
- *4 cups Swiss chard, roughly chopped*
- *butter*
- *salt & pepper to taste*
- *Honey Lavender Sauce (recipe follows)*
- *Goat Cheese Cakes (recipe follows)*

Preparation

HEAT oven to 150 degrees. Place duck breasts skin side down in a hot sauté pan and sear the skin side for about 3-4 minutes. Turn over and cook another 4-5 minutes until the duck is cooked to medium. Hold the duck in the warm oven while finishing the rest of the items.

SAUTÉ the Swiss chard until tender with butter, salt and pepper, and an ounce of water. To serve, place a portion of the sautéed Swiss chard onto the middle of the plate, and place a duck breast, cut in half, on top. Ladle with 1-2 ounces of the Honey Lavender Sauce and top with a Goat Cheese Cake. Enjoy.

Serves 4

For the Honey Lavender Sauce

- *1 small shallot, finely diced*
- *1 ounce apple cider vinegar*
- *½ cup honey*
- *1 cup chicken stock*
- *½ teaspoon lavender*
- *1 ounce white wine*
- *salt and pepper to taste*
- *cornstarch*

SAUTÉ shallots over medium heat until translucent. Deglaze with apple cider vinegar; reduce it by half, and add the honey, chicken stock, lavender, and white wine. Bring it to a boil and adjust the seasoning with salt and pepper. Thicken with cornstarch and keep warm until ready to serve.

For the Goat Cheese Cakes

- *4 ounces goat cheese*
- *1 egg white*
- *½ teaspoon flour*
- *salt & white pepper to taste*
- *½ cup untoasted small hazelnuts, crushed*

MIX the goat cheese, egg white, flour, and salt and white pepper. Form into 4 patties and coat with the crushed hazelnuts. In a sauté pan, sear the goat cheese cakes until brown on both sides and blot dry with a paper towel.

Seasons
Rotisserie & Grill
SEASONS
ROTISSERIE & GRILL
764 Main Avenue
Durango, CO 81301
970-382-9790
www.seasonsofdurango.com
Lunch Monday through Friday
11:30am – 2:30pm
Dinner Nightly from 5:30pm
Bar open 5:00pm

Seasons Rotisserie & Grill

Karen Barger, General Manager/Proprietor

Located in the heart of Durango, Seasons Rotisserie & Grill is the best place for watching the action on Main Avenue while enjoying a sumptuous meal in a bright and lively atmosphere. The dining room is bathed in warm tones of terracotta and ocher, with natural wood finishes and hand-wrought light fixtures. The centerpiece, though, is the open exhibition kitchen featuring a wood-burning grill and rotisserie. The dramatic high-energy bustle of a well-run kitchen radiates a contagious energy throughout the room, with Chef's Table seating offering an especially dramatic view of the culinary action.

Karen Barger has created a masterpiece of food and wine for Durango locals and visitors. Seasons' menu focuses on simple dishes prepared with exceptionally fresh ingredients. The warm, smoky flavors of the wood-burning grill impart a special flavor to many of the meats and vegetables. As true to its name, the menu changes with the seasons to take advantage of the best ingredients available at the time. But certain classics such as the rotisserie chicken, grilled bone-on ribeye, and the grilled double pork chop, remain year round by popular demand.

With close ties to the wine industry, wine is an integral part of Seasons' menu. The extensive list including a proprietor's page is easy to read, with interesting comments on the different varietals. The list has a wide-ranging choice of the best California wines, along with a large selection of international wines. To keep the wait staff educated about the different wines, managers hold daily pre-shift meetings and weekly wine education classes. Along with the investment in a superb cellar, this attention to the finer points of wine has earned the restaurant the *Wine Spectator's* coveted *Award of Excellence* every year since 2003.

With its emphasis on wine, Seasons has a wine cellar dining room that is available upon request for special occasions. Up to twenty guests can be seated at tables surrounded by marble and beautiful handmade mahogany bins. Special or limited menus are available, with the option to personalize. The restaurant also features special wine tastings in the room. Held once a month, "Eno-Tech" classes offer insights into wine and food pairings, cooking or preparation techniques, wine regions, styles or countries.

Award of Excellence

Butter Lettuce Salad

with Ginger-Plum Dressing

You may need more than one each of the mango, avocado, and red pepper, depending on their sizes. You will be dividing slices of these three between six plates, so judge your guests and their appetites.

Ingredients

- *3 hearts butter lettuce*
- *Ginger-Plum Dressing (recipe follows)*
- *1 large mango, peeled & sliced*
- *1 large avocado, peeled & sliced*
- *1 large red bell pepper, roasted & julienned*
- *¼ teaspoon toasted sesame seeds for garnish*
- *3 tablespoons unsalted toasted cashews*
- *6 tablespoons pickled ginger, as garnish*

Preparation

TEAR butter lettuce into large cups. Toss lettuce with Ginger-Plum Dressing, and then mound lettuce on plates. Alternate slices of mango, avocado, and julienned red pepper, and sprinkle with sesame seeds and toasted cashews. Top with a pickled ginger rosette.

For the Ginger-Plum Dressing

- *2 teaspoons fresh minced ginger*
- *2 teaspoons pickled ginger*
- *1 small egg yolk*
- *½ tablespoon soy sauce*
- *1½ tablespoons rice wine vinegar*
- *1½ tablespoons pineapple juice*
- *2 tablespoons plum sauce*
- *1 teaspoon chili-garlic paste*
- *1 ounce sesame oil*
- *3 ounces canola oil*
- *salt and pepper to taste*

COMBINE all ingredients, except the sesame and canola oils, in a food processor. With the food processor running, slowly drizzle in the oils. When all the oil is emulsified, taste and adjust the seasonings with salt and pepper.

Serves 6

Wine suggestion: Bonny Doon Pacific Rim Dry Riesling

Roasted Garlic Butternut Squash Soup

Ingredients

- 2 *large garlic heads, roasted, and puréed*
- *olive oil*
- 1 *large butternut squash (about 5 pounds)*
- *salt and pepper to taste*
- ½ *yellow onion, minced*
- ½ *cup white wine*
- 2 *quarts chicken stock*
- *lemon juice to taste*

Preparation

ROAST the garlic in olive oil in a small pot on the stove, cooking for a long time on very low heat until garlic is golden brown. The resulting garlic oil is wonderful used in many ways.

HEAT oven to 400 degrees. Cut squash in half lengthwise and remove seeds. Scrub with oil, preferably the oil used to roast the garlic. Season the squash with salt and pepper. Place squash face down on a baking sheet and bake until completely cooked, about 30 minutes. Scrape flesh of squash from skin, discarding skin.

IN A stockpot, sweat the onion in butter until translucent. Add garlic and squash purée. When they are both very hot, add white wine and cook until dry. Add chicken stock, and simmer for 45 minutes, stirring frequently. Purée the mixture, and then strain it. Season with salt, pepper, and lemon juice to adjust consistency.

Yield: about 2½ quarts

Wine suggestion: Zenato Pinot Grigio

Wild Mushroom Risotto

Ingredients

2 *quarts Wild Mushroom Stock (recipe follows)*
2 *cups, packed, of a variety of sliced mushrooms*
1 *teaspoon canola oil*
5 *tablespoons unsalted butter*
2 *medium onions, diced*
2 *cloves garlic, minced*
1 *sprig fresh thyme*
3 *cups Arborio rice*
1 *cup dry white wine*
½ *cup bleu cheese, crumbled*
salt and pepper to taste

Preparation

YOU will need two burners, side by side, 1 ladle, 1 wooden spoon, all the ingredients ready to use, about 20 minutes, and your undivided attention.

BRING 2 quarts of Wild Mushroom Stock to a simmer. In a pan or pot wide enough to accommodate the fire at a ½-inch depth, sauté the mushrooms on high heat in canola oil. The pan should be very hot in the beginning. Once the mushrooms have released their moisture, add 2 tablespoons of the butter and the minced onions. Cook until onions are translucent. Add garlic and thyme, cooking until the garlic is translucent and doesn't smell raw. Remove from pan and keep close at hand. Lower heat to medium. In the same pan, combine rice and two tablespoons of butter. Cook, stirring constantly until rice becomes translucent and smells toasty. Return mushroom mixture to the rice, add wine and cook, stirring constantly, until wine has completely evaporated.

ADD enough stock to cover the rice and cook, stirring constantly, until the stock has almost entirely evaporated. Repeat until rice is slightly al dente. When ready to serve, add one small ladle of stock. Add 1 tablespoon of butter and all the blue cheese, mixing until fully incorporated and the dish is creamy, not soupy. Season to taste with salt and pepper. Garnish each plate with fresh thyme.

For the Wild Mushroom Stock

2 *pounds button mushrooms*
1 *large onion*
1 *large carrot*
1 *large leek*
thyme stems
2 *bay leaves*
1 *tablespoon peppercorns*

GRIND mushrooms, plus any stems, then onion, carrot, and leek in a meat grinder. Sweat everything in a small amount of water until the juices are released. Cover with 2-3 gallons water and simmer for another hour, at least. Strain, cool, and reserve until use.

Serves 12

Wine suggestion: California Pinot Noir, such as AuBon Climat or Landmark.

Whole Roasted Pear with Cranberry Coulis

Ingredients

6 pears, peeled
2 tablespoons sugar
1 vanilla bean, split
3 tablespoons butter
pastry cream
Cranberry Coulis (recipe follows)

Preparation

HEAT oven to 300 degrees. Remove the core from the pears with a melon baller, leaving the stem on and the pear whole. In a pan that just fits them, arrange the pears upright and sprinkle with sugar. Put split vanilla bean on the bottom, in the middle. Break butter into small pieces and scatter it over the pears. Roast for 2-3 hours, basting frequently, until the pears are cooked through and starting to brown.

TO SERVE, place one dollop, about 1 tablespoon, of pastry cream in the center of each dish. Any simple pastry cream recipe will work for this. Pool the Cranberry Coulis around the plate, and perch the pear upright on the pastry cream, using the cream to hold the pear in place.

For the Cranberry Coulis

2 cups fresh whole cranberries
1 cup sugar
1 orange, juice of
orange zest
water to cover

COMBINE all ingredients in a small saucepan. The water should just cover the cranberries. Bring to a simmer, and cook for 20-30 minutes until cranberries are completely cooked. Blend and push through a strainer. If sauce is too thick, thin it with water. If sauce is too thin, simmer until the sauce reaches a consistency slightly thinner than desired.

Serves 6

Wine suggestion: Yalumba Antique Tawny Port or Belle de Brillet Pear Cognac

About the Publishers

Chuck and Blanche started Wilderness Adventures Press, Inc. in 1993, publishing outdoor and sporting books. Along with hunting and fishing, they love fine dining, good wines, and traveling. They have always been able to "sniff out" the most outstanding and interesting restaurants in any city they visit.

On weekends, they experiment in the kitchen, cooking a variety of fish and meats, as well as preparing the harvest from their time in the field. This love of cooking has resulted in a large library of cookbooks, and has inspired them to create a series of cookbooks based on their love of travel and fine dining.

Chuck and Blanche make their home in Gallatin Gateway, Montana, along with their four German wirehaired pointers.

Photo Copyrights/Credits

Front Cover, left to right: ©Hearthstone Restaurant; ©Blanche Johnson; ©L'Apogée; ©Tracy Johnson; ©Cottonwood Grill; © Denver Public Library, Western History Collection, Z-53; © Colorado Historical Society (Original photographs collection, CHS.X4676) All Rights Reserved; ©Tracy Johnson; ©Blanche Johnson; ©Ranch House Restaurant; © Denver Public Library, Western History Collection, George L. Beam, GB-7228; ©Mirabelle at Beaver Creek

Back Cover, left to right: ©Cazwellas; ©Metate Room; ©Mirabelle at Beaver Creek; ©Blanche Johnson; ©Alexander's; ©Mirabelle at Beaver Creek

All interior photos: ©Blanche T. Johnson or as noted below.

i: © Denver Public Library, Western History Collection, Mile High Photo Company, Z-7643; **vi, vii:** ©Tracy Jonhson; **viii (top):** © Denver Public Library, Western History Collection, Louis Charles McClure, MCC-2430; **vii (big):** © Colorado Historical Society (William Henry Jackson collection, CHS.J3890) All Rights Reserved; **xii (top):** © Denver Public Library, Western History Collection, Pat Coffey, X-1831; **xii (bottom):** © Colorado Historical Society (Original photographs collection, CHS.X4676) All Rights Reserved; **1-3:** ©L'Apogée; **7, 8, 13:** ©Cottonwood Grill; **14:** © Denver Public Library, Western History Collection, George L. Beam, GB-5181; **15, 16, 23:** ©Ranch House Restaurant; **25, 31, 32:** ©Tracy Johnson; **26:** ©Gasthaus Eichler; **36:** © Denver Public Library, Western History Collection, Clyde A. Jackson, Z-4337; **37, 38:** ©Champeaux; **41, 42, 45:** ©Great Northern Tavern; **48:** © Denver Public Library, Western History Collection, Z-53; **49, 50, 52:** ©Briar Rose Restaurant; **56:** © Denver Public Library, Western History Collection, Summit County Historical Society, X-991; **57-59, 64:** ©Hearthstone Restaurant; **65, 69, 70:** ©Tracy Johnson; **66:** ©St. Bernard; **71-73, 75:** ©Alexander's on the Creek; **76-78:** ©Tracy Johnson; **86:** © Denver Public Library, Western History Collection, Mac Julian, TMD-389; **88, 93:** ©Tracy Johnson; **98:** © Colorado Historical Society (Garrison collection, CHS.X6511) All Rights Reserved; **99, 100, 102, 105, 108:** ©Mirabelle; **109, 110:** ©Restaurant Six89; **119, 125:** ©Tracy Johnson; **124:** © Denver Public Library, Western History Collection, WPA Photo, X-6235; **132, 136:** ©Soupçon; **137-139:** ©Cazwellas; **142:** © Colorado Historical Society (William Henry Jackson Collection, CHS.J3130) All Rights Reserved; **143, 153:** ©Tracy Johnson; **144:** ©Remington's; **152:** © Denver Public Library, Western History Collection, Z-6288; **160:** © Denver Public Library, Western History Collection, George L. Beam, GB-7228; **166:** © Denver Public Library, Western History Collection, Joseph Collier, C-164; **167, 168, 171, 173:** ©9545 Restaurant; **175, 176:** ©Argentine Grill; **181-183:** ©Metate Room; **186:** © Denver Public Library, Western History Collection, George L. Beam, GB-7649; **187, 188, 195:** ©East by Southwest; **196:** Denver Public Library, Western History Collection, W. H. Jackson Photograph and Publishing Company, X-17602; **197:** ©Tracy Johnson; **203, 204:** ©Season's Rotisserie

Culinary Sources

This list is provided for your convenience. While many of the suggested suppliers have been recommended, not all suppliers have been individually checked out. We do not endorse any particular vendor or supplier.

Broken Arrow Ranch
Antelope, venison, wild boar, sausages
Ingram, TX
800-962-4263
www.brokenarrowranch.com

Chefshop.com
Gourmet foods, including pink salt.
www.chefshop.com

Dean and Deluca
Duck Confit, fine foods, kitchenware, gifts, wine.
Phone: 877-826-9246
www.deandeluca.com

Epicurious
Comprehensive website for recipes and culinary definitions
www.epicurious.com

Ethnic Grocer
Authentic foods from all over the world
Bensenville, IL
312-373-1777
www.ethnicgrocer.com

Gourmet Mushrooms and Products
Gourmet and organic mushrooms, growing kits
Graton, CA
800-789-9121
www.gmushrooms.com

Haystack Mountain
Award-winning farmstead goat cheese.
5239 Niwot Road
Niwot, CO 80503
Phone: 303-581-9948
www.haystackgoatcheese.com

Local Harvest
Locate food sources by state
www.localharvest.org

Maple Leaf Farms
Duck
800-382-5546 / 800-348-2812
www.mapleleaffarms.com

Oakwood Game Farms
Fresh & smoked gamebirds, wild rice
Princeton, MN
800-328-6647
www.oakwoodgamefarm.com

Penzey's Spices
Spices, herbs, and seasonings
800-741-7787
www.penzeys.com

Prairie Harvest Specialty Foods
Game meat, mushrooms, berries, foie gras
Spearfish, SD
800-350-7166
www.prairieharvest.com

Snake River Farms
Kobe beef and Kurobuta pork
Boise, ID
www.snakeriverfarms.com

Sweet Cactus Farms
Certified organic agave nectar.
10317 Washington Blvd.
Los Angeles, CA 90232
Phone: 310-733-4343
www.sweetcactusfarms.com

The Truffle Market
Fresh truffles, mushrooms, gourmet items
Gettysburg, PA
800-822-4003
www.trufflemarket.com

Valley Game & Gourmet
Game meats, foie gras, patés plus recipes
Wholesale site: www.valleygame.com
Retail site: www.dinewild.com

Glossary

al dente	Italian for "to the tooth", describing pasta or other food cooked only until it offers a slight resistance when bitten into, but which is not soft or overdone.
beurre noisette	A French term for butter cooked to a light brown color.
brioche	A French pastry bread made rich with butter and eggs that is used not only for desserts, but also in many meat and cheese dishes.
brunoise	A mixture of vegetables that have been finely diced or shredded, then cooked slowly in butter.
carpaccio	An Italian antipasto, usually consisting of very thin shavings of raw beef filet, drizzled with olive oil & lemon juice and garnished with capers or onions.
chiffonade	Similar to julienne, the process of cutting lettuce, endive, or herbs into thin even strips.
chinois	A very fine mesh cone-shaped metal sieve used for pureeing or straining. Often a spoon or pestle is used to press the food through it.
clarify	The process of clearing a cloudy substance, such as in stocks or wines, or of melting butter until the foam rises and is skimmed off.
concasse; concasser	A French term for chopping or pounding, often applied to tomatoes or herb mixtures.
cornichon	French for "gherkin" or small pickle.
coulis	A general term meaning a thick purée or sauce.
crème anglaise	A custard sauce with cream, sugar, egg yolks, and usually vanilla. It can be served either hot or cold, usually over cakes or fruit desserts.
demi-glace	A rich brown sauce (usually meat stock) combined with Madeira or sherry and slowly cooked until it's reduced by at least half, to a thick glaze.
dentelle	Thin slice of bread dried in a low temperature oven.
devein	To remove the blackish intestinal vein from the back of a shrimp with a sharp knife. The larger the shrimp, the more important it is to do this as the vein can contain grit.
emulsify	To blend together 2 or more liquids that do not naturally blend, such as oil and vinegar. Done by whisking the ingredients together with an emulsifier such as an egg yolk or milk.
foie gras	A gourmet food product usually made from the liver of geese or ducks that have been force-fed and not allowed to exercise. The liver is then soaked overnight, marinated in wine or brandy and then baked.
frizzle	To fry until crisp and curled over high heat.
gastrique	A mixture of vinegar and sugar that is reduced until almost evaporated. Usually used in sauces made with fruit.
gavi	dry white wine made from the cortese grape in Italy
julienne	A method of cutting vegetables into thin strips, usually about 1 inch by 1/16 inch.
kosher salt	An additive-free coarse-grained salt.
lardons; lardoons	A French term for narrow strips of fat used to lard meats, sometimes used for bacon that has been diced, blanched, and fried.

masa harina	A cornflour used in Mexican dishes. Corn is processed with lime to remove hull, then ground and dried.
micro carnival amaranth	Amaranth is a high protein green similar in flavor to spinach. Micro refers to a specific size of amaranth, and carnival is a mix of particularly colorful amaranth leaves that has a great visual effect.
mirin	A sweet, rice wine used in cooking to sweeten meat or fish dishes.
mole	A smooth, cooked blend of onion, garlic, chilies, ground pumpkin or sesame seeds, and a small amount of Mexican chocolate.
mount, to	A cooking technique in which small, cold, unsalted butter chunks are whisked into a sauce just before serving.
nappe	A term indicating the thickness of a liquid, usually described as thick enough to coat the back of a spoon.
panko	Coarse Japanese bread crumbs used for coating fried foods.
papillote	A greased parchment paper packet in which food is baked and served.
phyllo; filo	Thin layers of pastry dough used in sweet and savory recipes.
pink salt	A flaky salt with a fragrant but mild flavor and apricot to pink in color. Excellent as a finishing salt, it gets its color from a red algae in the evaporation ponds.
prosciutto	Italian word for ham that is seasoned, salt-cured, air-dried, but not smoked.
quenelle	A light dumpling made of minced or ground fish, meat, or vegetables, seasoned and bound with eggs. The mixture is formed into small ovals and gently poached in stock.
remouillage	A second rendering of meat bones that have already been used to make stock. Weaker than the first stock, it is often reduced to make a glaze.
rondeau	A straight-sided, round, shallow pan with a lid and two handles.
roux	A mixture of equal parts flour and butter used to thicken sauces. Cooking different lengths of time results in different flavors and colors.
sambal oelek	A condiment popular in Indonesia and southern India, it is usually made with chiles, brown sugar, and salt. It usually accompanies rice and curried dishes.
scald	To heat a liquid to just below the boiling point. Usually done to milk.
semifreddo	An Italian word meaning "half cold". Refers to a chilled or partially frozen dessert.
silver skin	A thin, tough, membrane found on meat that will cause the meat to curl when cooked if not removed.
slurry	A thin mixture of water and flour or cornstarch used as a thickener.
sweat	To cook vegetables slowly in a tightly covered pan so that they literally stew in their own juice.
temper	To warm beaten eggs by stirring a little of the hot ingredients into them before adding the eggs to the entire hot ingredients. This keeps the eggs from solidifying.
truffle	A fungus that is cultivated primarily in France and Italy, valued for its earthy, aromatic nature.
truffle oil	Created when truffles are soaked in olive oil.
turbinado sugar	Steam-cleaned raw sugar, blond in color with a slight molasses flavor.
wasabi	Sometimes called Japanese horseradish, this green-colored condiment comes in paste and powder form.

Index

Symbols

9545 Restaurant 167

A

Alexander's on the Creek 71
Almond Rice Pilaf 148
Appetizer
- Beet Marinated Salmon 96
- Carpaccio di Bue (Beef Carpaccio) 121
- Colorado Corn and Crab Cake 183
- Cottonwood Shrimp and Crab Cakes 9
- Crab Cakes with Remoulade 59
- Duck Cakes 155
- Escargot in Sauce Persillé 79
- Escargot with Maitre d' Butter 51
- Jumbo Lump Crab Cakes over Wilted Spinach 163
- Lobster Au Gratin 3
- Lobster Spring Rolls 128
- Mahi Mahi "Dorado" Ceviche 190
- Maine Lobster Meatballs 44
- Masa-Crusted Crisp Crab Cakes 178
- Prince Edward Island Mussels 73
- Rhubarb Martini 111
- Seared Hudson Valley Foie Gras 133
- Shrimp Calvados 52
- Smoked Salmon Tartare 27
- Spring Vegetable & Chorizo Beggar's Purse 145
- Stuffed Calamari 43
- Torchon of Foie Gras 80
- Warm Pistachio Crusted Haystack Mountain Goat Cheese 89

Apple & Jalapeno Chutney 193
Apple Strudel 30
Apple Vanilla Rum Sauce 5
Apricot (or peach) Tartelette 107
Apricot Shallot Glaze 170
Argentine Grille 175
Artichoke Ceviche 127
Artichoke Ravioli 103
Asparagus Soup with Truffle Oil 95

B

Baby Creamer Potatoes 83
Baked Tomato Spinach Mousse 150
Beano's Cabin 93
Beef & Veal
- Beef Teriyaki Skewers "Yakitori" 194
- Blanquette of Veal 54
- Carpaccio di Bue (Beef Carpaccio) 121
- Grilled "Gaucho Style" Beef Tenderloin 179
- Grilled Filet Mignon 149
- Harvest Beef Tender Stew 201
- Kobe Beef-wrapped Asparagus 189
- Roast Beef Wellington 97
- Roasted Beef Tenderloin 165
- Slow Roasted Niman Ranch Tenderloin 21
- Steak Au Poivre 61
- Sweetbreads in Caper Brown Butter Sauce 84
- Veal Saltimbocca 29

Beef Teriyaki Skewers "Yakitori" 194
Beet Marinated Salmon 96
Berries & Choya with Ginger Ice Cream 195
Berry Salsa 20
Black Bean Sauce 193
Blackberry Demi-Glace 62
Black Pepper Pappardelle 115
Blanquette of Veal 54
Blueberry Corn Cakes 116
Brandy Mustard Sauce 61
Briar Rose Restaurant 49
Brie Salad 67
Broiled Duck Breast 202
Brown Butter Sauce 82
Butter Lettuce Salad 205
Butternut Squash Soup 145

C

Campo de Fiori 119
Caramel Semifreddo 117
Carpaccio di Bue (Beef Carpaccio) 121
Cazwellas 137
Champagne Dijon Cream Sauce 163
Champeaux 37
Charred Tomato Beurre Blanc 164
Cherry Glaze 12
Cherry Merlot Sauce 13
Chicken Marsala 70
Chilean Sea Bass "Miso Yaki" 191
Chipotle Ketchup 43
Chive Oil 146
Chocolate Fondant 107

Cilantro Cream 178
Cilantro Curry Sauce 11
Cilantro Pesto 177
Cinnamon Dusted Elk Tenderloin 129
Cipollini Onions 85
Citrus Beurre Blanc 169
Colorado Corn & Beet Salad 40
Colorado Corn and Crab Cake 183
Colorado Lamb and Goat Cheese "Stroganoff" 90
COTTONWOOD GRILL 7
Cottonwood Shrimp and Crab Cakes 9
Crab Cakes with Remoulade 59
Cranberry Coulis 208
Creamy Seafood Chowder 96
Crispy Carrots 169
Croissant Bread Pudding
and Apple Compote 174
Cucumber Sunomono Salad 194

D

Dark Chocolate Pot Du Crème 47
DESSERTS
- Apple Strudel 30
- Apricot (or peach) Tartelette 107
- Berries & Choya with Ginger Ice Cream 195
- Blueberry Corn Cakes 116
- Caramel Semifreddo 117
- Chocolate Fondant 107
- Croissant Bread Pudding and Apple Compote 174
- Dark Chocolate Pot Du Crème 47
- Dessert Trio 107
- Flan 141
- Ginger Wild Blueberry Sorbet 151
- Raspberry White Chocolate Bread Pudding 63
- Root Beer Poached Pears 117
- Soupçon Crème Brûlée 136
- Sweet Corn Ice Cream 116
- Swiss Tart with Colorado Peaches 23
- Toasted Coconut Cheesecake 6
- Tropical Trifle 107
- Vanilla Bean Crème Brûlée 75
- Whole Roasted Pear with Cranberry Coulis 208

Dessert Trio 107
Diver Sea Scallops 169
Dover Sole 101
Dover Sole Meunière 82
DRESSINGS, MARINADES, & RUBS
- Chive Oil 146
- Ginger-Plum Dressing 205
- Opal Basil Emulsion 40
- Oregano Vinaigrette 112
- Passion Fruit Vinaigrette 17
- Pomegranate Vinaigrette 81
- Raspberry Vinaigrette 67
- Rosemary Lemon Vinaigrette 33
- Sherry Vinaigrette 159
- Tarragon Dijon Dressing 199

Duck Cakes 155
Duck Confit 158

E

EAST BY SOUTHWEST 187
Edamame Purée 46
Elk Mountain Mushroom Mix 157
Escargot in Sauce Persillé 79
Escargot with Maitre d' Butter 51

F

Farfalle al Salmone 123
Fennel and Grapefruit Salad 199
Fig-Port Purée 133
FISH, SEAFOOD
- Beet Marinated Salmon 96
- Chilean Sea Bass "Miso Yaki" 191
- Colorado Corn and Crab Cake 183
- Cottonwood Shrimp and Crab Cakes 9
- Crab Cakes with Remoulade 59
- Creamy Seafood Chowder 96
- Diver Sea Scallops 169
- Dover Sole 101
- Dover Sole Meunière 82
- Escargot in Sauce Persillé 79
- Escargot with Maitre d' Butter 51
- Farfalle al Salmone 123
- Grilled Ruby Red Trout 164
- Grilled Shrimp with Marinated Tomatoes 39
- Jumbo Lump Crab Cakes over Wilted Spinach 163
- Lobster Au Gratin 3
- Lobster Spring Rolls 128
- Mahi Mahi "Dorado" Ceviche 190
- Maine Lobster Meatballs 44
- Masa-Crusted Crisp Crab Cakes 178
- Mustard-Dusted Ruby Red Trout 40
- Pan-seared Atlantic Halibut 134

Pan Seared Halibut 34
Prince Edward Island Mussels 73
Rainbow Trout over Shiitake Salad 128
Rock Shrimp and Brie Stuffed Halibut 147
Rock Shrimp Hash 135
Sake-Lime Marinated Chilean Sea Bass 10
Sautéed Halibut Filet 103
Seafood Cannelloni 68
Seared Halibut 127
Sea Scallops 104
Shrimp Calvados 52
Smoked Salmon Tartare 27
Southwestern Salmon Tamales 200
Spice Grilled Tuna 60
Stuffed Calamari 43
Stuffed Colorado Striped Bass 53
Trout with Warm Tomato Salsa 19
Turbotin 105
Yellow Fin Tuna 102
Flan 141
FOWL
Broiled Duck Breast 202
Chicken Marsala 70
Duck Cakes 155
Duck Confit 158
Maple Leaf Farm Duckling 134
Seared Hudson Valley Foie Gras 133
Torchon of Foie Gras 80
Twice Roasted Chinese Five Spice Peking Duck 12
French Bean Salad 146
Fresh Tomato Gazpacho Sauce 200

G

GAME
Broiled Duck Breast 202
Cinnamon Dusted Elk Tenderloin 129
Duck Cakes 155
Duck Confit 158
Garlic Granola Crusted Elk Chop 62
Grilled Antelope with Prickly Pear Sauce 22
Herb Marinated Bone-in Elk Loin 91
Hickory Smoked Buffalo Ribeye 185
Jack Daniels Marinated Caribou 130
Maple Leaf Farm Duckling 134
Pan Seared Elk Tenderloin 74
Pheasant Crepe 159
Rabbit and Mushroom Ragout 114
Twice Roasted Chinese Five Spice Peking Duck 12
Wild Mushroom Brandied Elk Tenderloins 55
Garlic Granola Crusted Elk Chop 62
GASTHAUS EICHLER 25
Ginger-Plum Dressing 205
Ginger Pear Chutney 171
Ginger Wild Blueberry Sorbet 151
Goat Cheese-Fig Orzo 34
Goat Cheese Cakes 202
Goat Cheese Gnocchi over Field Greens 111
Goat Cheese Stroganoff 90
Golden Raisins in Plum Wine Syrup 89
Gorgonzola Mashers 150
Gorgonzola Sauce 185
GREAT NORTHERN TAVERN 41
Green Curry Coconut Soba Noodles 10
Grilled "Gaucho Style" Beef Tenderloin 179
Grilled Antelope with Prickly Pear Sauce 22
Grilled Asparagus 74
Grilled Filet Mignon 149
Grilled Onions 91
Grilled Pork Chop 140
Grilled Pork Chops 113
Grilled Pork Chops with Berry Salsa 20
Grilled Ruby Red Trout 164
Grilled Shrimp with Marinated Tomatoes 39

H

Harvest Beef Tender Stew 201
Haystack Mountain Goat Cheese Crusted Colorado Lamb Rack 172
HEARTHSTONE RESTAURANT 57
Herb Marinated Bone-in Elk Loin 91
Hickory Smoked Buffalo Ribeye 185
Hoisin Ginger Marinated Pork Tenderloin 11
Honey Lavender Sauce 202
Horseradish Cream Sauce 21
Horseradish Potato 97
Hot Portabella Mushroom Salad 17

I

Insalata Panzanella 33
Insalata Pazza 122

J

Jack Daniels Marinated Caribou 130
Jicama-Apple Slaw 178

Jicama Salsa 139
Jumbo Lump Crab Cakes over Wilted Spinach 163

K

Kobe Beef-wrapped Asparagus 189
Kurobuta Pork Chop Adobo 192
Kurobuta Pork Chops 5

L

L'Apogée 1
Lamb
Colorado Lamb and Goat Cheese "Stroganoff" 90
Goat Cheese Stroganoff 90
Haystack Mountain Goat Cheese Crusted Colorado Lamb Rack 172
Mint Tea Marinated Lamb Loin 46
Rack of Lamb 106
La Tour 77
Lobster Au Gratin 3
Lobster Cream Sauce 68
Lobster Demi-glace 44
Lobster Spring Rolls 128

M

Madeira Sauce 83
Mahi Mahi "Dorado" Ceviche 190
The Mahogany Grille 197
Maine Lobster Meatballs 44
Mango Lime Sauce 6
Maple Anglaise 118
Maple Leaf Farm Duckling 134
Masa-Crusted Crisp Crab Cakes 178
Metate Room 181
Micro Amaranth Salad 81
Mint Tea Marinated Lamb Loin 46
Mirabelle Restaurant at Beaver Creek 99
Miso Beurre Blanc 128
Mushroom Onion Soup 156
Mustard-Dusted Ruby Red Trout 40
Myer's Rum Caramel Sauce 63

N

Northern Bean and Root Vegetable Ragout 92

O

Olathe Sweet Corn Bisque 177
Onion Rings 165
Opal Basil Emulsion 40
Oregano Vinaigrette 112

P

Pan-seared Atlantic Halibut 134
Pan Seared Elk Tenderloin 74
Pan Seared Halibut 34
Pappardelle Tartufo Bianco 69
Parsley Chimichurri 179
Passion Fruit Vinaigrette 17
Pasta
Artichoke Ravioli 103
Black Pepper Pappardelle 115
Farfalle al Salmone 123
Goat Cheese-Fig Orzo 34
Goat Cheese Stroganoff 90
Pappardelle Tartufo Bianco 69
Seafood Cannelloni 68
Peach Bourbon BBQ Sauce 113
Persimmon Marmalade 81
Pheasant Crepe 159
Pico de Gallo 190
Pine Creek Cookhouse 125
Plum Ginger Lacquer 135
Pomegranate Syrup 129
Pomegranate Vinaigrette 81
Pork
Grilled Pork Chop 140
Grilled Pork Chops 113
Grilled Pork Chops with Berry Salsa 20
Hoisin Ginger Marinated Pork Tenderloin 11
Kurobuta Pork Chop Adobo 192
Kurobuta Pork Chops 5
Sake Marinated, Apricot Kurobuta Pork Tenderloin 170
Tuscan Stuffed Pork Loin 35
Port Reduction Sauce 165
Port Wine and Paonia Cherry Reduction 173
Potato Pavé 129
Prickly Pear Sauce 22
Prince Edward Island Mussels 73

R

Rabbit and Mushroom Ragout 114
Rack of Lamb 106
Rainbow Trout over Shiitake Salad 128
RANCH HOUSE RESTAURANT 15
Raspberry Vinaigrette 67
Raspberry White Chocolate Bread Pudding 63
Ratatouille over Polenta 18
Red Beets 89
Red Wine Sauce 97
REMINGTON'S 143
Remoulade 59
RESTAURANT SIX89 109
Rhubarb Martini 111
RICE, GRAINS, & BEANS
  Almond Rice Pilaf 148
  Green Curry Coconut Soba Noodles 10
  Northern Bean and Root Vegetable Ragout 92
  Roasted Pine Nut Risotto 5
  Rosemary Pine Nut Risotto 164
  Smoked Mozz Grits 113
  Spätzle 28
  Sun-Dried Tomato and Pine Nut Pilaf 36
  Wild Mushroom Risotto 207
Roast Beef Wellington 97
Roasted Beef Tenderloin 165
Roasted Garlic-Eggplant and Brie Soup 184
Roasted Garlic Butternut Squash Soup 206
Roasted Garlic Yukon Gold Mashed Potatoes 193
Roasted Jalapeno Béarnaise 149
Roasted Pine Nut Risotto 5
Roasted Red Pepper Coulis 163
Rock Shrimp and Brie Stuffed Halibut 147
Rock Shrimp Hash 135
Root Beer Poached Pears 117
Rosemary Lemon Vinaigrette 33
Rosemary Pine Nut Risotto 164

S

Sage Madeira Cream 35
Sake-Lime Marinated Chilean Sea Bass 10
Sake Marinated, Apricot Kurobuta
  Pork Tenderloin 170
SALADS
  Brie Salad 67
  Butter Lettuce Salad 205
  Colorado Corn & Beet Salad 40
  Cucumber Sunomono Salad 194
  Fennel and Grapefruit Salad 199
  French Bean Salad 146
  Goat Cheese Gnocchi over Field Greens 111
  Hot Portabella Mushroom Salad 17
  Insalata Panzanella 33
  Insalata Pazza 122
  Jicama-Apple Slaw 178
  Micro Amaranth Salad 81
  Rainbow Trout over Shiitake Salad 128
  Sizzle Salad 4
Salsa alle Erbe Fini 121
SAUCES, SALSAS, & CHUTNEYS
  Apple & Jalapeno Chutney 193
  Apple Vanilla Rum Sauce 5
  Apricot Shallot Glaze 170
  Berry Salsa 20
  Black Bean Sauce 193
  Blackberry Demi-Glace 62
  Brandy Mustard Sauce 61
  Brown Butter Sauce 82
  Champagne Dijon Cream Sauce 163
  Charred Tomato Beurre Blanc 164
  Cherry Glaze 12
  Cherry Merlot Sauce 13
  Chipotle Ketchup 43
  Cilantro Cream 178
  Cilantro Curry Sauce 11
  Cilantro Pesto 177
  Citrus Beurre Blanc 169
  Cranberry Coulis 208
  Fig-Port Purée 133
  Fresh Tomato Gazpacho Sauce 200
  Ginger Pear Chutney 171
  Golden Raisins in Plum Wine Syrup 89
  Gorgonzola Sauce 185
  Honey Lavender Sauce 202
  Horseradish Cream Sauce 21
  Jicama Salsa 139
  Lobster Cream Sauce 68
  Lobster Demi-glace 44
  Madeira Sauce 83
  Mango Lime Sauce 6
  Maple Anglaise 118
  Miso Beurre Blanc 128
  Myer's Rum Caramel Sauce 63
  Parsley Chimichurri 179
  Peach Bourbon BBQ Sauce 113
  Persimmon Marmalade 81

Pico de Gallo 190
Plum Ginger Lacquer 135
Pomegranate Syrup 129
Port Reduction Sauce 165
Port Wine and Paonia Cherry Reduction 173
Prickly Pear Sauce 22
Red Wine Sauce 97
Remoulade 59
Roasted Jalapeno Béarnaise 149
Roasted Red Pepper Coulis 163
Sage Madeira Cream 35
Salsa alle Erbe Fini 121
Soy Glacé 60
Sun-Dried Cherry Bordelaise 92
Sun-dried Tomato Pesto Butter 148
Tarragon Beurre Blanc 34
Warm Tomato Salsa 19
Wasabi Aioli 9
Wasabi Beurre Blanc 60
Watercress Coulis 103
Watercress Sauce 127
Sautéed Halibut Filet 103
Seafood Cannelloni 68
Seared Halibut 127
Seared Hudson Valley Foie Gras 133
Sea Scallops 104
SEASONS ROTISSERIE & GRILL 203
Sherry Vinaigrette 159
Shrimp Calvados 52
SIDE DISHES
Artichoke Ceviche 127
Baby Creamer Potatoes 83
Baked Tomato Spinach Mousse 150
Cipollini Onions 85
Crispy Carrots 169
Edamame Purée 46
Elk Mountain Mushroom Mix 157
Goat Cheese-Fig Orzo 34
Goat Cheese Cakes 202
Gorgonzola Mashers 150
Grilled Asparagus 74
Grilled Onions 91
Horseradish Potato 97
Jicama-Apple Slaw 178
Northern Bean and Root Vegetable Ragout 92
Onion Rings 165
Potato Pavé 129
Ratatouille over Polenta 18
Red Beets 89
Roasted Garlic Yukon Gold Mashed Potatoes 193
Rock Shrimp Hash 135
Smoked Mozz Grits 113
Spätzle 28
Spring Vegetable & Chorizo Beggar's Purse 145
Sweet Potato Lasagne 130
Toasted Brioche 81
Tomato Tartar 147
Truffled Mashed Potatoes 74
Wilted Spinach 148
Sizzle Salad 4
Slow Roasted Niman Ranch Tenderloin 21
Smoked Mozz Grits 113
Smoked Salmon Tartare 27
SOUPÇON 131
Soupçon Crème Brûlée 136
SOUPS
Asparagus Soup with Truffle Oil 95
Black Bean Sauce 193
Butternut Squash Soup 145
Creamy Seafood Chowder 96
Mushroom Onion Soup 156
Olathe Sweet Corn Bisque 177
Roasted Garlic-Eggplant and Brie Soup 184
Roasted Garlic Butternut Squash Soup 206
Wild Mushroom Stock 207
Southwestern Salmon Tamales 200
Soy Glacé 60
Spätzle 28
Spice Grilled Tuna 60
Spring Vegetable & Chorizo Beggar's Purse 145
ST. BERNARD 65
Steak Au Poivre 61
Stuffed Calamari 43
Stuffed Colorado Striped Bass 53
Sun-Dried Cherry Bordelaise 92
Sun-Dried Tomato and Pine Nut Pilaf 36
Sun-dried Tomato Pesto Butter 148
Sweetbreads in Caper Brown Butter Sauce 84
Sweet Corn Ice Cream 116
Sweet Potato Lasagne 130
Swiss Tart with Colorado Peaches 23

T

TARRAGON AT ELK MOUNTAIN RESORT 153
Tarragon Beurre Blanc 34

Tarragon Dijon Dressing 199
Terra Bistro 87
The Shed Restaurant 31
The Wine Spectator Award 24
Toasted Brioche 81
Toasted Coconut Cheesecake 6
Tomato Tartar 147
Torchon of Foie Gras 80
Tropical Trifle 107
Trout with Warm Tomato Salsa 19
Truffled Mashed Potatoes 74
Tundra Restaurant 161
Turbotin 105
Tuscan Stuffed Pork Loin 35
Twice Roasted Chinese Five Spice Peking Duck 12

V

Vanilla Bean Crème Brûlée 75
Veal Saltimbocca 29

W

Warm Pistachio Crusted Haystack Mountain Goat Cheese 89
Warm Tomato Salsa 19
Wasabi Aioli 9
Wasabi Beurre Blanc 60
Watercress Coulis 103
Watercress Sauce 127
Whole Roasted Pear with Cranberry Coulis 208
Wild Mushroom Brandied Elk Tenderloins 55
Wild Mushroom Risotto 207
Wild Mushroom Stock 207
Wilted Spinach 148

Y

Yellow Fin Tuna 102